SPRI

AWAKENING

by

FRANK WEDEKIND

COMPASS CIRCLE

Spring Awakening.
Written by Frank Wedekind.
Translated by Francis J. Ziegler.
Current edition published by Compass Circle in 2020.

Published by Compass Circle
Cover copyright ©2020 by Compass Circle.

Note:
All efforts have been made to preserve original spellings and punctuation of the original edition which may include old-fashioned English spellings of words and archaic variants.

This book is a product of its time and does not reflect the same views on race, gender, sexuality, ethnicity, and interpersonal relations as it would if it were written today.

For information contact :
information@compass-circle.com

I didn't ask to be born, and I don't owe God anything.

FRANK WEDEKIND

SECRET WISDOM OF THE AGES SERIES

Life presents itself, it advances in a fast way. Life indeed never stops. It never stops until the end. The most diverse questions peek and fade in our minds. Sometimes we seek for answers. Sometimes we just let time go by.

The book you have now in your hands has been waiting to be discovered by you. This book may reveal the answers to some of your questions.

Books are friends. Friends who are always by your side and who can give you great ideas, advice or just comfort your soul.

A great book can make you see things in your soul that you have not yet discovered, make you see things in your soul that you were not aware of.

Great books can change your life for the better. They can make you understand fascinating theories, give you new ideas, inspire you to undertake new challenges or to walk along new paths.

Literature Classics like the one of *Spring Awakening* are indeed a secret to many, but for those of us lucky enough to have discovered them, by one way or another, these books can enlighten us. They can open a wide range of possibilities to us. Because achieving greatness requires knowledge.

The series SECRET WISDOM OF THE AGES presented by Compass Circle try to bring you the great timeless masterpieces of literature, autobiographies and personal development,.

We welcome you to discover with us fascinating works by Nathaniel Hawthorne, Sir Arthur Conan Doyle, Edith Wharton, among others.

- exploration   • adolescent, exploration
- questioning
- education
- innocence vs experience vs ignorance

A PROEM FOR PRUDES

THAT it is a fatal error to bring up children, either boys or girls, in ignorance of their sexual nature is the thesis of Frank Wedekind's drama *"Frühlings Erwachen."* From its title one might suppose it a peaceful little idyl of the youth of the year. No idea a could be more mistaken. It is a tragedy of frightful import, and its action is concerned with the development of natural instincts in the adolescent of both sexes.

The playwright has attacked his theme with European frankness; but of plot, in the usual acceptance of the term, there is little. Instead of the coherent drama of conventional type, Wedekind has given us a series of loosely connected scenes illuminative of character—scenes which surely have profound significance for all occupied in the training of the young. He sets before us a group of school children, lads and lassies just past the age of puberty, and shows logically that death and degradation may be their lot as the outcome of parental reticence. They are not vicious children, but little ones such as we meet every day, imaginative beings living in a world of youthful ideals and speculating about the mysteries which surround them. Wendla, sent to her grave by the abortive administered with the connivance of her affectionate but mistaken mother, is a most lovable creature, while Melchior, the father of her unborn child, is a high type of boy whose downfall is due to a philosophic temperament, which leads him to inquire into the nature of life and to impart his knowledge to others; a temperament which, under proper guidance, would make him a useful, intelligent man. It is Melchior's very excellence of character which proves his undoing. That he should be imprisoned as a moral degenerate only serves to illustrate the stupidity of his parents and teachers. As for the suicide of Moritz, the imaginative youth who kills himself because he has failed in his examinations, that is another crime for which the dramatist makes false educational methods responsible.

A grim vein of humor is exhibited now and then, as when we are introduced to the conference room in which the members of a gymnasium faculty, met to consider the regulation of their pupils' morals, sit beneath the portraits of Pestalozzi and J. J. Rousseau disputing with considerable acrimony about the opening and shutting of a window. The exchange of unpleasant personalities is interrupted only by the entrance of the accused

1

student, to whose defense the faculty refuses to listen, having marked the boy for expulsion prior to the formal farce of his trial.

Wedekind has been accused of depicting his adults as too ignorant and too indifferent to the needs of the younger generation. But most of us will have to admit that the majority of his scenes and characters seem very true to life.

"*Frühlings Erwachen*" may not be pleasant reading exactly, but there is no forgetting it after one has perused it; there is an elemental strength about it which grips the intellect. As a play it stands unique in the annals of dramatic art. That it has succeeded in attracting much attention abroad is shown by the fact that this drama in book form has gone through twenty-six editions in its original version and has been translated into several European tongues, Russian included, while stage performances of the work have been given in France as well as in Germany.

The Teutonic grimness of the work puzzled the Parisians, who are not used to having philosophy thrust at them over the footlights; but in Germany "*Frühlings Erwachen*" proved much more successful. In Berlin, indeed, it has become part of the regular stock of plays acted at "*Das Neue Theater*," where it is said to be certain of drawing a crowded audience. That the play is radically different from anything given on the American stage is undoubtedly true. It must be remembered, however, that the Continental European playwright regards the stage as a medium of instruction, as well as a place of amusement. The dictum of the Swedish dramatist, August Strindberg, that the playwright should be a lay priest preaching on vital topics of the day in a way to make them intelligible to mediocre intellects, is not appreciated in this country as it should be; but once admit the kinship of dramatist and priest, and the position taken by Wedekind in writing "*Frühlings Erwachen*" becomes self-evident. There should be no question concerning the importance of his topic, nor should it be forgotten that the evident lesson he seeks to inculcate is one now preached by numerous ethical teachers. In order to estimate the relationship of this play toward modern thought in Germany, it must be understood that Wedekind's tragedy is merely one of the documents in a paper war which has resulted at last in having the physiology of sex taught in many German schools. The fact that Wedekind's dialogue is frank to a remarkable degree only makes his preachment more effective: "One does not cure the pest with attar of roses," as St. Augustine remarked.

Conditions in this country are not so very different from those depicted in this play, and evidence is not lacking that gradually, very gradually, we are beginning to realize that ignorance and innocence are not synonymous; that an evil is not palliated by ignoring its existence; the Podsnappian wave of the hand has not disappeared entirely, but it is not quite as fashionable as of yore. All things considered, the moment seems appropriate for the publication, of "*Frühlings Erwachen*" in an English version. The translation given in this volume follows the German original as closely as the translator can reconcile the nature of the two languages.

Considered as a work of literature, "*Frühlings Erwachen*" is remarkable as one of the few realistic studies of adolescence. Its deceptive simplicity is the hall mark of that supreme literary ability which knows how to conceal art by art. Dealing with adolescence, an unformed period of human life, it is necessarily without the climaxes we expect in dramas in which the characters are adult, and the gruesome scene in the churchyard with which the play closes—a scene with such peculiar symbolism could spring only from a Teutonic imagination—leaves much unended.

It is interesting to note, by the way, that Wedekind himself appears as the Masked Man when "*Frühlings Erwachen*" is given in Berlin, a fact which gives this scene somewhat the nature of a *parabasis*. direct address

Frank Wedekind's name is just beginning to be heard in America. In Germany he has been recognized for some time as one of the leaders in the new art of the theatre. Naturally enough, his plays are too outspoken in their realism to appeal to all his fellow-countrymen. But, if certain Germans reject this mental pabulum, others become intoxicated by it, and, waxing enthusiastic with a flow of language almost bacchic, hail Wedekind as the forerunner of a new drama—as a power destined to infuse fresh strength into the German stage. "With this drink in its body," writes one admirer, "the public will never more endure lyrical lemonade, nor the dregs of dramatic penury."

Again, these enthusiasts compare Wedekind's work to that of the pre-Shakesperian dramatists, or even to that of the Bard of Avon himself, both of which comparisons are difficult to grasp by an English-speaking student of the British drama.

Wedekind, it is true, has a habit of using the news of the day as material for plays, just as the old English dramatists did when they wrote "domestic tragedies." He has a fondness, moreover, for gruesome situations such as we can imagine appealing to the melancholy genius of Webster; but of the childlike simplicity which marks much of the Elizabethan drama there is not a particle.

Certainly there is no trace of the gentle romanticism which one finds in some of the other modern German realists. Gerhart Hauptmann can turn from the grim task of dramatizing starvation, as he does in *"Die Weber,"* to indulge in the naïve Christian symbolism of *"Hannele,"* or the mythological poetry of *"Die Versunkene Glocke."* Even the iconoclast Strindberg writes romantically at times, and gives us something resembling Maeterlinck; but when Wedekind departs from pure realism his fancy creates a Gothic nightmare of horrors, peopled with such terrifying creatures as the headless suicide wandering amid the graves.

Wedekind's kinship to the dramatists of the "domestic tragedies" is shown clearly in the tragedy *"Musik,"* which deals with a phase of music study only too common in Germany. It is asserted that of the thousands of students of music in that country not one in a hundred amounts to anything artistically, while of those who master their art not one in a thousand is capable of profiting financially by it. It is this condition of affairs which gives additional importance to this recent work of Wedekind.

"Musik" is described by the author as a depiction of morals in four pictures (*"Sittengemälde in vier Bildern"*), to each of which he has given a separate title, a method which enables him to indulge in his trick of applying a pretty, inoffensive name to a tragic subject, as he does in picture two of this series, which he calls "Behind Swedish Curtains," and which represents the interior of a jail. The curtains to which the playwright refers are the iron bars of the prison.

The central character in *"Musik,"* Klara Huhnerwadel, is a neurotic girl, whose mad love for her singing teacher has entangled her in the meshes of the legal net drawn to catch Madame Fischer, a notorious character in real life, who actively engaged the attention of the German police authorities not long ago. At the instigation of her lover, Josef Reissner, and with money supplied by Else Reissner, Josef's wife, Klara flees to Antwerp, only to find existence insupportable there, and to return to a life in jail which drives her to the edge of insanity. Released from imprisonment, she continues her relationship with her teacher until their association becomes public scandal, and then takes refuge in the country, intending to devote her life to her illegitimate child. The child dies, however, and there descends upon Klara what Wedekind describes as "the curse of the ridiculous." In an outburst of frightful anguish she is filled with "a nameless loathing of the horrible fate of being racked to death by bursts of sneering laughter," and

4

raves in hysteria by the bedside of her dead baby.

Upon this final picture Wedekind has expended his full power of biting irony. Josef Reissner, the cause of Klara's misfortune, is thanked by her mother for all he has done for her, while Franz Lindekuh, a literary man, whose rôle in the play has been that of a good Samaritan, is accused as the author of her disgrace. During previous tribulations Reissner has assured Klara repeatedly that her suffering would develop her artistic temperament and result in bringing her fame as a singer. At the end, when Klara, after undergoing imprisonment, exile, poverty, public disgrace and the loss of her beloved child, finds herself bereft of even Reissner's regard, she is led away in a stupor from her miserable attic. It is then, in reply to a wish of the physician that she will suffer from no lasting mental disturbance, that Lindekuh preludes the fall of the curtain by the caustic remark: "She'll be able to sing a song."

Here, truly, is a tragedy! There can be no doubt but what Wedekind has handled it in a powerful fashion. He sounds the tragic note upon the first rising of the curtain, a note which grows in intensity until the auditor wonders if it is possible for it to reach higher——and yet it swells.

"*Frühlings Erwachen*" is the best known of the Wedekind dramas and the most original in its treatment. It has peculiarities, however, which make it somewhat difficult to give as a stage performance. To see what this German playwright can do on more conservative lines, and to appreciate his mastership of the conventional technique of the stage, one must turn to the dramas of modern life in which he handles such subjects as socialism, woman's emancipation, naturalism and divorce; frequently, it must be confessed, in a way which Americans refuse to tolerate upon the stage, despite their fondness for the same sort of information when supplied by the newspapers.

Selecting his characters from all classes of life, Wedekind brings to their making the knowledge of life as the police reporter sees it plus the science of a skilled psychologist. There is something sardonic about his art. He does not appear to sympathize with any of his characters, but to stand outside of life making note of the foibles and failures of his fellow-creatures. His irony appears in the most tragic places, and his dialogue, wrought with a cunning which requires strict attention on the part of the auditor if its subtleties would be grasped, serves Wedekind as an instrument for dissecting souls which he wields quite regardless of the mess he may make in the operating room.

None knows better how to show the peculiarities of a neurotic woman, or to betray a man's weakness by a few short sentences. The demonstration is direct and thorough, and we watch it fascinated, as we might the work of a skilled vivisectionist. When the job is finished we feel convinced that Wedekind's personages are real, although many of them are not the kind we enjoy meeting in actual life. We do meet them daily, nevertheless, tolerating them chiefly by our own polite habit of ascribing imaginary virtues to those that possess them not.

Take that curious comedy, *"Der Marquis von Keith,"* as an example of Wedekind's skill as a psychologist. "Comedy" the author names it himself, but he might just as well have called it a tragic farce, so thoroughly has he mingled the laughable with the tragic. The protagonist of this peculiar play (the underlying tone of which has been likened musically to a Dies Irae written by Offenbach) is the illegitimate son of a teacher of mathematics and a gypsy trull, an adventurer who keeps on the shady side of the law, and who, despite his practical view of life in general, is an idealist in several particulars. His title of Marquis von Keith is merely a *nom de guerre*, and his attempts to obtain a fortune involve methods which the world acclaims as evidences of wonderful financial ability, or stigmatizes as the practices of a sharper, according to their success or failure. Resourceful, energetic, unhampered by vain regrets or restrictions of conventional morals, wasting not a moment upon a scheme which has proved unprofitable, von Keith is a forceful personage who manages to pass in Munich as a wealthy American, even when his pockets are empty and the sheriff is at the door. His own view of life is embodied in his definition of sin as "the mythological symbol for bad business," and his accompanying explanation that good business can be conducted only by a person accepted by the existing order of society.

In other words, von Keith is a hypocrite for revenue only, but never is deceived concerning his own personality.

The play deals with von Keith's scheme to build an amusement hall, to be known as "The Fairy Palace." He applies himself so sedulously that his plans are on the eve of realization, when suddenly he finds himself ousted from the management of his own enterprise by the very men he has interested in it.

Now all this is comedy, of course, but Wedekind is not to be deprived of his predelection for the minor key. He introduces the tragic tone in this instance right in the final scene, when von Keith is confronted by the dead body of his common-law wife, Molly Griefinger. In some respects this

6

episode resembles a travesty upon the final act of Sudermann's "*Sodoms Ende*;" but it is characteristic of Wedekind that he makes Molly kill herself because she fears von Keith's success will estrange her from her husband, and that her suicide is followed directly by the failure of von Keith's well-laid plans, just as they seemed about to mature.

It is characteristic, also, that the crowd which denounces von Keith as the cause of Molly's death, and which threatens to do him bodily harm, is composed of tradesmen whose initial cause of discontent is to be found in the promoter's failure to pay his bills.

Wedekind's certainty of touch is as much in evidence in his handling of his minor characters as it is in the portrayal of von Keith. There is Molly, whose little bourgeois soul fears the great world, shrinks from her husband's acquaintances, and dreads to take its place among the wealthy classes; Simba, the artist's model, who is astonished at anybody pitying her as a victim of civilization when she can get drunk on champagne; Casimir, the wealthy merchant; and the Bohemian painter Saranieff, with his friend Zamrjaki, the composer. As an antithesis to von Keith we are introduced to Ernst Scholz, a weakling whose soul is torn by internal strife, until its owner is at peace neither with himself nor the world. Scholz wastes his time seeking a reason for his own existence and in longing to become a useful member of society; von Keith scorns to bother his brain with such trifles, boldly proclaiming the Nietzschean doctrine that the only way to be useful to others is to help one's self as much as possible, and asserting that he would rather gather cigar stumps in the café gutters than live in slothful peace in the country. There is no doubt about von Keith being a rogue, in the conventional acceptance of the term, but his enthusiasm appeals to us and we feel for him in his undoing at the end of the play.

In "*Die Junge Welt*" Wedekind shows us the laughable attempts of a party of young girls to live a life of celibacy in pursuance of a resolution taken in boarding school. It is an amusing comedy, and contains, among other interesting personages, a literary man, who nearly drives his wife to divorce by his habit of jotting down notes of her emotions, even when he is kissing her.

An opportunity to comment upon the German *lese majesty* is not neglected by Wedekind in the romantic drama, "*So ist das Leben*," a dignified and carefully wrought work, partly in verse, which deals with the tribulations of a deposed monarch in his own country. This exiled king becomes tramp, tailor and strolling player, to end eventually as court jester of the very man who has taken his place on the throne.

"*Der Kammersänger*," three scenes from the life of a popular tenor, is little more than a dramatic sketch. "*Der Erdgeist*" and "*Die Büchse der Pandora*," two plays which constitute an integral whole, deal with a lady who embraces Mrs. Warren's profession. These, with "*Der Leibestrank*" and "*Oaha*," two farces, with traces of real psychology, round out the total of Wedekind's dramatic works. In addition, he has indulged in verse-making and written a number of short stories somewhat in the manner of De Maupassant.

One may feel at times that Wedekind's art would gain by the exercise of more restraint, but there is no denying it is a great relief from "lyric lemonade."

An attempt to explain symbolism is usually a dangerous matter. If a failure, it makes the one who essays the task ridiculous. If successful, it cheapens the value of the symbolism; symbolism being a kind of an overtone to verbal reasoning, to which it bears much the same relationship as music does to poetry. In spite of this double danger, the translator ventures to close this review with a guess at the personality of the Masked Man who plays such an important part in the final scene of "*Frühlings Erwachen*" and to whom the author has dedicated the play. To the translator, then, this mysterious personage is none other than Life, Life in its reality, not Life as seen through the fogged glasses of Melchior's pedagogues or the purblind eyes of the unfortunate mother who sends her daughter to an untimely grave.

FRANCIS J. ZIEGLER.

June, 1909.

ACT I

SCENE FIRST.

A Dwelling Room.

WENDLA.

Why have you made my dress so long, Mother?

FRAU BERGMANN.

You are fourteen years old to-day.

WENDLA.

Had I known you were going to make my dress so long, I would rather not have been fourteen.

FRAU BERGMANN.

The dress is not too long,

WENDLA.

What do you want? Can I help it that my child is two inches taller every spring? As a grown-up maiden you cannot go about in short dresses.

WENDLA.

At any rate, my short dress becomes me better than this nightgown.—Let me wear it again, Mother, only through this summer. This penitential robe will fit me just as well whether I am fifteen or fourteen. Let's put it aside until my next birthday, now I should only tear the flounces.

FRAU BERGMANN.

I don't know what to say. I want to take special care of you just now, child. Other girls are hardy and plump at your age. You are the contrary.——Who knows what you will be when the others have developed?

9

WENDLA.

Who knows—possibly I shall not be at all.

FRAU BERGMANN.

Child, child, how do such thoughts come to you!

WENDLA.

Don't, dear Mother, don't be sad.

FRAU BERGMANN.

(*Kissing her.*)
My own darling!

WENDLA.

They come to me at night when I can't sleep. I am not made sad by them, and I believe that I sleep better after them. Is it sinful, Mother, to have such thoughts?

FRAU BERGMANN.

Go hang the long dress up in the closet. Put on your short dress again, in God's name!—I will put another depth of ruffles on it.

WENDLA.

(*Hanging the dress in the closet.*)
No, I would rather be twenty at once——!

FRAU BERGMANN.

If only you are not too cold!——The dress was long enough for you in its time, but——

WENDLA.

Now, when summer is coming?——Mother, when one is a child, one doesn't catch diphtheria in one's knees! Who would be so cowardly. At my age one doesn't freeze—least of all in the legs. Would it be any better for me to be too warm, Mother? Give thanks to God if some day your darling doesn't tear out the sleeves and come to you at twilight without her shoes and stockings!—If I wore my long dress I should dress like an elfin queen under it.—Don't scold, Mother! Nobody sees it any more.

SCENE SECOND.

Sunday Evening.

MELCHIOR.

This is too tiresome for me. I won't do anything more with it.

OTTO.

Then we others can stop, too!——Have you the work, Melchior?

MELCHIOR.

Keep right on playing!

MORITZ.

Where are you going?

MELCHIOR.

For a walk.

GEORGE.

But it's growing dark!

ROBERT.

Have you the work already?

MELCHIOR.

Why shouldn't I go walking in the dark?

ERNEST.

Central America!——Louis the Fifteenth!——Sixty verses of Homer!—— Seven equations!

MELCHIOR.

Damn the work!

11

GEORGE.

If only Latin composition didn't come to-morrow!

MORITZ.

One can't think of anything without a task intervening.

OTTO.

I'm going home.

GEORGE.

I, too, to work.

ERNEST.

I, too, I too.

ROBERT.

Good-night, Melchior.

MELCHIOR.

Sleep well! (*All withdraw save Moritz and Melchior.*) I'd like to know why we really are on earth!

MORITZ.

I'd rather be a cab-horse than go to school!——Why do we go to school?——We go to school so that somebody can examine us!——And why do they examine us?——In order that we may fail. Seven must fail, because the upper classroom will hold only sixty.——I feel so queer since Christmas.——The devil take me, if it were not for Papa, I'd pack my bundle and go to Altoona to-day!

MELCHIOR.

Let's talk of something else——
(*They go for a walk.*)

MORITZ.

Do you see that black cat there with its tail sticking up?

MELCHIOR.

Do you believe in omens?

MORITZ.

I don't know exactly. They come down to us. They don't matter.

MELCHIOR.

I believe that is the Charybdis on which one runs when one steers clear of the Scylla of religious folly.——Let's sit down under this beech tree. The cool wind blows over the mountains. Now I should like to be a young dryad up there in the wood to cradle myself in the topmost branches and be rocked the livelong night.

MORITZ.

Unbutton your vest, Melchior.

MELCHIOR.

Ha!——How clothes make one puff up!

MORITZ.

God knows, it's growing so dark that one can't see one's hand before one's eyes. Where are you?——Do you believe, Melchior, that the feeling of shame in man is only a product of his education?

MELCHIOR.

I was thinking over that for the first time the day before yesterday. It seems to me deeply rooted in human nature. Only think, you must appear entirely clothed before your best friend. You wouldn't do so if he didn't do the same thing.——Therefore, it's more or less of a fashion.

MORITZ.

I have often thought that if I have children, boys and girls, I will let them occupy the same room; let them sleep together in the same bed, if possible; let them help each other dress and undress night and morning. In hot weather, the boys as well as the girls, should wear nothing all day long but a short white woolen tunic with a girdle.——It seems to me that if they grew up that way they would be easier in mind than we are under the present regulations.

MELCHIOR.

I believe so decidedly, Moritz!——The only question is, suppose the girls have children, what then?

MORITZ.

How could they have children?

MELCHIOR.

In that respect I believe in instinct. I believe, for example, that if one brought up a male and a female cat together, and kept both separated from the outside world——that is, left them entirely to their own devices——that, sooner or later, the she cat would become pregnant, even if she, and the tom cat as well, had nobody to open their eyes by example.

MORITZ.

That might happen with animals——

MELCHIOR.

I believe the same of human beings. I assure you, Moritz, if your boys sleep in the same bed with the girls, and the first emotion of manhood comes unexpectedly to them—I should like to wager with anyone——

MORITZ.

You may be right—but after all——

MELCHIOR.

And when your girls reached the same age it would be the same with them! Not that the girls exactly—one can't judge that the same, certainly—at any rate, it is supposable—and then their curiosity must not be left out of account.

MORITZ.

A question, by the way——

MELCHIOR.

Well?

MORITZ.

But you will answer?

MELCHIOR.

Naturally!

MORITZ.

Truly?!

MELCHIOR.

My hand on it.——Now, Moritz?

MORITZ.

Have you written your composition yet??

MELCHIOR.

Speak right out from your heart!——Nobody sees or hears us here.

MORITZ.

Of course, my children will have to work all day long in yard or garden, or find their amusement in games which are combined with physical exercise. They must ride, do gymnastics, climb, and, above all things, must not sleep as soft as we do. We are weakened frightfully.——I believe one would not dream if one slept harder.

MELCHIOR.

From now until fall I shall sleep only in my hammock. I have shoved my bed back of the stove. It is a folding one. Last winter I dreamed once that I flogged our Lolo until he couldn't move a limb. That was the most gruesome thing I ever dreamed.——Why do you look at me so strangely?

MORITZ.

Have you experienced it yet?

MELCHIOR.

What?

MORITZ.

How do you say it?

MELCHIOR.

Manhood's emotion?

MORITZ.

M—'hm.

MELCHIOR.

Certainly!

MORITZ.

I also —— —— —— —— —— —— —— —— —— —— —— —— ——
—— —— ——

MELCHIOR.

I've known that for a long while!——Almost for a year.

MORITZ.

I was startled as if by lightning.

hot dreams?

MELCHIOR.

Did you dream?

MORITZ.

Only for a little while—of legs in light blue tights, that strode over the
teacher's desk—to be correct, I thought they wanted to go over it. I only
saw them for an instant.

MELCHIOR.

George Zirschnitz dreamed of his mother.

MORITZ.

Did he tell you that?

MELCHIOR.

Out there on the gallow's road.

MORITZ.

If you only knew what I have endured since that night!

MELCHIOR.

Qualms of conscience?

MORITZ.

Qualms of conscience??——The anguish of death!

MELCHIOR.

Good Lord——

MORITZ.

I thought I was incurable. I believed I was suffering from an inward hurt.—
—Finally I became calm enough to begin to jot down the recollections
of my life. Yes, yes, dear Melchior, the last three weeks have been a
Gethsemane for me.

MELCHIOR.

I was more or less prepared for it when it came. I felt a little ashamed of myself.——But that was all.

MORITZ.

And yet you are a whole year younger than I am.

MELCHIOR.

I wouldn't bother about that, Moritz. All my experience shows that the appearance of this phantom belongs to no particular age. You know that big Lämmermeier with the straw-colored hair and the hooked nose. He is three years older than I am. Little Hans Rilow says Lämmermeier dreams now only of tarts and apricot preserves.

MORITZ.

But, I ask you, how can Hans Rilow know that?

MELCHIOR.

He asked him.

MORITZ.

He asked him?——I didn't dare ask anybody.

MELCHIOR.

But you asked me.

MORITZ.

God knows, yes!——Possibly Hans, too, has made his will.——Truly they play a remarkable game with us. And we're expected to give thanks for it. I don't remember to have had any longing for this kind of excitement. Why didn't they let me sleep peacefully until all was still again. My dear parents might have had a hundred better children. I came here, I don't know how, and must be responsible because I didn't stay away.—— Haven't you often wondered, Melchior, by what means we were brought into this whirl?

MELCHIOR.

Don't you know that yet either, Moritz?

MORITZ.

How should I know it? I see how the hens lay eggs, and hear that Mamma
had to carry me under her heart. But is that enough?——I remember,
too, when I was a five year old child, to have been embarrassed when
anyone turned up the décolleté queen of hearts. This feeling has disappeared. At the same time, I can hardly talk with a girl to-day without
thinking of something indecent, and—I swear to you, Melchior—I don't
know what.

MELCHIOR.

I will tell you everything. I have gotten it partly from books, partly from
illustrations, partly from observations of nature. You will be surprised;
it made me an atheist. I told it to George Zirschnitz! George Zirschnitz
wanted to tell it to Hans Rilow, but Hans Rilow had learned it all from
his governess when he was a child.

MORITZ.

I have gone through Meyer's Little Encyclopedia from A to Z. Words—
nothing but words and words! Not a single plain explanation. Oh, this
feeling of shame!——What good to me is an encyclopedia that won't
answer me concerning the most important question in life?

MELCHIOR.

Did you ever see two dogs running together about the streets?

MORITZ.

No!——Don't tell me anything to-day, Melchior. I have Central America
and Louis the Fifteenth before me. And then the sixty verses of Homer,
the seven equations and the Latin composition.——I would fail in all of
them again to-morrow. To drudge successfully I must be as stupid as
an ox.

MELCHIOR.

Come with me to my room. In three-quarters of an hour I will have the Homer, the equations and two compositions. I will put one or two harmless errors in yours, and the thing is done. Mamma will make lemonade for us again, and we can chat comfortably about propagation.

MORITZ.

I can't——I can't chat comfortably about propagation! If you want to do me a favor, give me your information in writing. Write me out what you know. Write it as briefly and clearly as possible, and put it between my books to-morrow during recess. I will carry it home without knowing that I have it. I will find it unexpectedly. I cannot but help going over it with tired eyes——in case it is hard to explain, you can use a marginal diagram or so.

MELCHIOR.

You are like a girl.——Nevertheless, as you wish. It will be a very interesting task for me.——One question, Moritz?

MORITZ.

Hm?

MELCHIOR.

Did you ever see a girl?

MORITZ.

Yes!

MELCHIOR.

All of her?

MORITZ.

Certainly!

20

MELCHIOR.

So have I!——Then we won't need any illustrations.

MORITZ.

During the Schützenfest in Leilich's anatomical museum! If it had leaked out I should have been hunted out of school.——Beautiful as the light of day, and——oh, so true to nature!

MELCHIOR.

I was at Frankfurt with Mamma last summer——Are you going already, Moritz?

MORITZ.

I must work.——Good-night.

MELCHIOR.

'Till we meet again.

SCENE THIRD.

Thea, Wendla and Martha come along the street arm in arm.

MARTHA.

How the water gets into one's shoes!

WENDLA.

How the wind blows against one's cheeks!

THEA.

How one's heart thumps!

WENDLA.

Let's go out there to the bridge. Ilse says the stream is full of bushes and trees. The boys have built a raft. Melchi Gabor was almost drowned yesterday.

THEA.

Oh, he can swim!

MARTHA.

I should think so, child!

WENDLA.

If he hadn't been able to swim he would have been drowned!

THEA.

Your hair is coming down, Martha, your hair is coming down.

MARTHA.

Pooh!——Let it come down! It bothers me day and night. I may not wear short hair like you; I may not wear my hair down my back like Wendla; I may not wear bangs, and I must always do my hair up at home——all on account of my aunt!

WENDLA.

I'll bring the scissors with me to-morrow to devotions. While you are saying, "Blessed are they who do not stray," I will clip it off.

MARTHA.

For heaven's sake, Wendla! Papa would beat me black and blue, and Mamma would lock me up in the coal hole for three nights.

WENDLA.

What does he beat you with, Martha?

MARTHA.

It often seems to me as if they would miss something if they didn't have an ill-conditioned brat like me.

THEA.

Why, girl!

MARTHA.

Are you ever allowed to put a blue ribbon through the top of your chemise?

THEA.

A pink ribbon! Mamma thinks a pink ribbon goes well with my big dark eyes.

MARTHA.

Blue suits me to a T!——Mamma pulled me out of bed by the hair. I fell with my hands out so on the floor.——Mamma prayed night after night with us——

WENDLA.

In your place I should have run away long ago.

MARTHA.

There you have it! The reason I am going away!——There you have it!—— They will soon see——oh, they will soon see! At least I shall never be able to reproach my mother——

THEA.

H'm, h'm.——

MARTHA.

Can you imagine, Thea, what Mamma meant by it?

THEA.

I can't——can you, Wendla?

WENDLA.

I should simply have asked her.

MARTHA.

I lay on the floor and shrieked and howled. Then Papa came in. Rip——he tore off my chemise. Out of the door I went. There you have it!——I only wanted to get out in the street that way——

WENDLA.

But that is not so, Martha.

MARTHA.

I froze. I was locked up. I had to sleep all night in a sack.

THEA.

Never in my life could I sleep in a sack!

WENDLA.

I only wish I could sleep once for you in your sack.

MARTHA.

If only one weren't beaten!

THEA.

But one would suffocate in it!

MARTHA.

Your head is left outside. It's tied under your chin.

THEA.

And then they beat you?

MARTHA.

No. Only when there is special occasion.

WENDLA.

What do they beat you with, Martha?

MARTHA.

Oh, with anything that is handy.——Does your mother think it's naughty to eat a piece of bread in bed?

WENDLA.

No! no!

MARTHA.

I believe they enjoy it——even if they don't say so. If I ever have children I will let them grow up like the weeds in our flower garden. Nobody worries about them and they grow so high and thick——while the roses in the beds grow poorer and poorer every summer.

THEA.

If I have children I shall dress them all in pink. Pink hats, pink dresses, pink shoes. Only the stockings——the stockings shall be black as night! When I go for a walk they shall march in front of me.——And you, Wendla?

WENDLA.

How do you know that you will have any?

THEA.

Why shouldn't we have any?

MARTHA.

Well, Aunt Euphemia hasn't any.

THEA.

You goose, that's because she isn't married.

WENDLA.

Aunt Bauer was married three times and she didn't have a single one.

MARTHA.

If you have any, Wendla, which would you rather have, boys or girls?

WENDLA.

Boys! boys!

THEA.

I, too, boys!

MARTHA.

So would I. Better twenty boys than three girls.

THEA.

Girls are tiresome.

MARTHA.

If I weren't a girl already I certainly wouldn't want to be one.

WENDLA.

That's a matter of taste, I believe, Martha. I rejoice every day that I am a girl. Believe me, I wouldn't change places with a king's son.——That's the reason why I only want boys!

THEA.

But that's crazy, pure craziness, Wendla!

WENDLA.

But it must be a thousand times more exciting to be loved by a man than by a girl!

THEA.

But you don't want to assert that Forest Inspector Pfälle loves Melitta more than she does him.

WENDLA.

That I do, Thea. Pfälle is proud. Pfälle is proud because he is a forest inspector—for Pfälle has nothing.——Melitta is happy because she gets ten thousand times more than she is.

MARTHA.

Aren't you proud of yourself, Wendla?

WENDLA.

That would be silly.

MARTHA.

In your place I should be proud of my appearance.

THEA.

Only look how she steps out——how free her glance is—how she holds herself, Martha. Isn't that pride?

WENDLA.

Why not? I am so happy to be a girl; if I weren't a girl I should break down the next time——
(*Melchior passes and greets them.*)

THEA.

He has a wonderful head.

MARTHA.

He makes me think of the young Alexander going to school to Aristotle.

THEA.

Oh dear, Greek history!——I only know how Socrates lay in his barrel when Alexander sold him the ass' shadow.

WENDLA.

He stands third in his class.

THEA.

Professor Knochenbruch says he can be first if he wants.

MARTHA.

He has a beautiful brow, but his friend has a soulful look.

THEA.

Moritz Stiefel?——He's a stupid!

MARTHA.

I've always gotten along well with him.

THEA.

He disgraces anybody who is with him. At Rilow's party he offered me some bon-bons. Only think, Wendla, they were soft and warm. Isn't that——? He said he had kept them too long in his trouser's pocket.

WENDLA.

Only think, Melchi Gabor told me once that he didn't believe anything—— not in God, not in a hereafter——in anything more in this world.

SCENE FOURTH.

A park in front of the grammar school. Melchior, Otto, George, Robert, Hans Rilow and Lämmermeier.

MELCHIOR.

Can any of you say where Moritz Stiefel is keeping himself?

GEORGE.

It may go hard with him!——Oh, it may go hard with him!

OTTO.

He'll keep on until he gets caught dead to rights.

LAEMMERMEIER.

Lord knows, I wouldn't want to be in his skin at this moment!

ROBERT.

What cheek! What insolence!

MELCHIOR.

Wha——Wha——what do you know?

GEORGE.

What do we know?——Now, I tell you——

LAEMMERMEIER.

I wish I hadn't said anything!

OTTO.

So do I——God knows I do!

MELCHIOR.

If you don't at once——

ROBERT.

The long and the short of it is, Moritz Stiefel has broken into the Board
Room.

MELCHIOR.

Into the Board Room——?

OTTO.

Into the Board Room. Right after the Latin lesson.

GEORGE.

He was the last. He hung back intentionally.

LAEMMERMEIER.

As I turned the corner of the corridor, I saw him open the door.

MELCHIOR.

The devil take——

LAEMMERMEIER.

If only the devil doesn't take him.

GEORGE.

Perhaps the Rector didn't take the key.

ROBERT.

Or Moritz Stiefel carries a skeleton key.

OTTO.

That may be possible.

LAEMMERMEIER.

If he has luck, he'll only be kept in.

ROBERT.

Besides getting a demerit mark in his report!

OTTO.

If this doesn't result in his being kicked out.

HANS RILOW.

There he is!

MELCHIOR.

White as a handkerchief.
(*Moritz comes in in great agitation.*)

LAEMMERMEIER.

Moritz, Moritz, what have you done!

MORITZ.

Nothing——nothing——

ROBERT.

You're feverish!

MORITZ.

From good fortune——from happiness——from jubilation——

OTTO.

You were caught!

MORITZ.

I am promoted!——Melchior, I am promoted! Oh, I don't care what
happens now!——I am promoted!——Who would have believed that
I should be promoted!——I don't realize it yet!——I read it twenty
times!——I couldn't believe it——Good Lord, it's so!——It's so; I am
promoted! (*Laughing.*) I don't know——I feel so queer——the ground
turns around——Melchior, Melchior, can you realize what I've gone
through?

HANS RILOW.

I congratulate you, Moritz——Only be happy that you got away with it!

MORITZ.

You don't know, Hans, you can't guess, what depends on it. For three weeks
I've slunk past that door as if it were a hellish abyss. To-day I saw it was
ajar. I believe that if some one had offered me a million——nothing, oh
nothing, could have held me.——I stood in the middle of the room,—
I opened the report book——ran over the leaves——found——and
during all that time——I shudder——

MELCHIOR.

——During all that time?

MORITZ.

During all that time the door behind me stood wide open. How I got
out——how I came down the steps, I don't know.

HANS RILOW.

Is Ernest Röbel promoted, too?

MORITZ.

Oh, certainly, Hans, certainly!——Ernest Röbel is promoted, too.

ROBERT.

Then you can't have read correctly. Counting in the dunce's stool, we, with you and Robert, make sixty-one, and the upper class-room cannot accommodate more than sixty.

MORITZ.

I read it right enough. Ernest Röbel is given as high a rating as I am—both of us have conditions to work off.——During the first quarter it will be seen which of us has to make room for the other. Poor Röbel!—— Heaven knows, I'm not afraid of myself any longer. I've looked into it too deeply this time for that.

OTTO.

I bet five marks that you lose your place.

MORITZ.

You haven't anything. I won't rob you.——Lord, but I'll grind from to-day on!——I can say so now——whether you believe it or not——It's all the same now——I——I know how true it is; if I hadn't been promoted I would have shot myself.

ROBERT.

Boaster!

GEORGE.

Coward!

OTTO.

I'd like to see you shoot yourself!

LAEMMERMEIER.

Box his ears.

MELCHIOR.

(*Gives him a cuff.*)
Come, Moritz, let's go to the forester's house!

GEORGE.

Do you believe his nonsense?

MELCHIOR.

What's that to you? Let them chatter, Moritz! Come on, let's go to town. (*Professors Hungergurt and Knochenbruch pass by.*)

KNOCHENBRUCH.

It is inexplicable to me, my dear colleague, how the best of my scholars can fail the very worst of all.

HUNGERGURT.

To me, also, professor.

SCENE FIFTH.

A sunny afternoon—Melchior and Wendla meet each other in the wood.

MELCHIOR.

Is it really you, Wendla?——What are you doing up here all alone?——For three hours I've been going from one side of the wood to the other without meeting a soul, and now you come upon me out of the thickest part of it!

WENDLA.

Yes, it's I.

MELCHIOR.

If I didn't know you were Wendla Bergmann, I would take you for a dryad, fallen out of your tree.

WENDLA.

No, no, I am Wendla Bergmann.——How did you come here?

MELCHIOR.

I followed my thoughts.

WENDLA.

I'm hunting waldmeister.[1] Mamma wants to make Maybowl. At first she intended coming along herself, but at the last moment Aunt Bauer dropped in, and she doesn't like to climb.——So I came by myself.

MELCHIOR.

Have you found your waldmeister?

WENDLA.

A whole basketful. Down there under the beach it grows as thick as meadow clover. Just now I am looking for a way out. I seem to have lost the path. Can you tell me what time it is?

MELCHIOR.

Just a little after half-past four. When do they expect you?

WENDLA.

I thought it was later. I lay dreaming for a long time on the moss by the brook. The time went by so fast, I feared it was already evening.

MELCHIOR.

If nobody is waiting for you, let us linger here a little longer. Under the oak tree there is my favorite place. If one leans one's head back against the trunk and looks up through the branches at the sky, one becomes hypnotized. The ground is warm yet from the morning sun.——For weeks I've been wanting to ask you something, Wendla.

---

[1]An aromatic herb, used in preparing a beverage drunk in Spring time.

WENDLA.

But I must be home at five o'clock.

MELCHIOR.

We'll go together, then. I'll take the basket and we'll beat our way through the bushes, so that in ten minutes we'll be on the bridge!——When one lies so, with one's head in one's hand, one has the strangest thoughts.——

(*Both lie down under the oak.*)

WENDLA.

What do you want to ask me, Melchior?

MELCHIOR.

I've heard, Wendla, that you visit poor people's houses. You take them food and clothes and money also. Do you do that of your own free will, or does your mother send you?

WENDLA.

Mother sends me mostly. They are families of day laborers that have too many children. Often the husband can't find work and then they freeze and go hungry. We have a lot of things which were laid away long ago in our closets and wardrobes and which are no longer needed.——But how did you know it?

MELCHIOR.

Do you go willingly or unwillingly, when your mother sends you?

WENDLA.

Oh, I love to go!——How can you ask?

MELCHIOR.

But the children are dirty, the women are sick, the houses are full of filth, the men hate you because you don't work——

WENDLA.

That's not true, Melchior. And if it were true, I'd go just the same!

MELCHIOR.

Why just the same, Wendla?

WENDLA.

I'd go just the same! It would make me all the happier to be able to help them.

MELCHIOR.

Then you go to see the poor because it makes you happy?

WENDLA.

I go to them because they are poor.

MELCHIOR.

But if it weren't a pleasure to you, you wouldn't go?

WENDLA.

Can I help it that it makes me happy?

MELCHIOR.

And because of it you expect to go to heaven! So it's true, then, that which has given me no peace for a month past!—Can the covetous man help it that it is no pleasure to him to go to see dirty sick children?

WENDLA.

Oh, surely it would give you the greatest pleasure!

MELCHIOR.

And, therefore, he must suffer everlasting death. I'll write a paper on it and send it to Pastor Kahlbauch. He is the cause of it. Why did he fool us with the joy of good works.—If he can't answer me I won't go to Sunday-school any longer and won't let them confirm me.

WENDLA.

Why don't you tell your trouble to your dear parents? Let yourself be confirmed, it won't cost you your head. If it weren't for our horrid white dresses and your long trousers one might be more spiritual.

MELCHIOR.

There is no sacrifice! There is no self-denial! I see the good rejoice in their hearts, I see the evil tremble and groan—I see you, Wendla Bergmann, shake your locks and laugh while I am as melancholy as an outlaw.— What did you dream, Wendla, when you lay in the grass by the brook?

WENDLA.

——Foolishness——nonsense.——

MELCHIOR.

With your eyes open?

WENDLA.

I dreamed I was a poor, poor beggar girl, who was turned out in the street at five o'clock in the morning. I had to beg the whole long day in storm and bad weather from rough, hard-hearted people. When I came home at night, shivering from hunger and cold, and without as much money as my father coveted, then I was beaten——beaten——

MELCHIOR.

I know that, Wendla. You have the silly children's stories to thank for that. Believe me, such brutal men exist no longer.

WENDLA.

Oh yes, Melchior, you're mistaken. Martha Bessel is beaten night after night, so that one sees the marks of it the next day. Oh, but it must hurt! It makes one boiling hot when she tells it. I'm so frightfully sorry for her that I often cry over it in my pillows at night. For months I've been thinking how one can help her.——I'd take her place for eight days with pleasure.

MELCHIOR.

One should complain of her father at once. Then the child would be taken away from him.

WENDLA.

I, Melchior, have never been beaten in my life——not a single time. I can hardly imagine what it means to be beaten. I have beaten myself in order to see how one felt then in one's heart——It must be a gruesome feeling.

MELCHIOR.

I don't believe a child is better for it.

WENDLA.

Better for what?

MELCHIOR.

For being beaten.

WENDLA.

With this switch, for instance! Ha! but it's tough and thin.

MELCHIOR.

That would draw blood!

WENDLA.

Would you like to beat me with it once?

MELCHIOR.

Who?

WENDLA.

Me.

MELCHIOR.

What's the matter with you, Wendla?

WENDLA.

What might happen?

MELCHIOR.

Oh, be quiet! I won't beat you.

WENDLA.

Not if I allow you?

MELCHIOR.

No, girl!

WENDLA.

Not even if I ask you, Melchior?

MELCHIOR.

Are you out of your senses?

WENDLA.

I've never been beaten in my life!

MELCHIOR.

If you can ask for such a thing——

WENDLA.

Please——please——

MELCHIOR.

I'll teach you to say please! (*He hits her.*)

WENDLA.

Oh, Lord, I don't notice it in the least!

MELCHIOR.

I believe you——through all your skirts——

WENDLA.

Then strike me on my legs!

MELCHIOR.

Wendla! (*He strikes her harder.*)

WENDLA.

You're stroking me! You're stroking me!

MELCHIOR.

Wait, witch, I'll flog Satan out of you!

(*He throws the switch aside and beats her with his fists so that she breaks out with a frightful cry. He pays no attention to this, but falls upon her as if he were crazy, while the tears stream heavily down his cheeks. Presently he springs away, holds both hands to his temples and rushes into the depths of the wood crying out in anguish of soul.*)

ACT II

SCENE FIRST.

Evening in Melchior's study. The window is open, a lamp burns on the table.—Melchior and Moritz on the divan.

MORITZ.

Now I'm quite gay again, only a little bit excited.——But during the Greek lesson I slept like the besotted Polyphemus. I'm astonished that the pronunciation of the ancient tongue doesn't give me the earache.——To-day I was within a hair of being late——My first thought on waking was of the verbs in μι——Himmel—Herrgott—Teufel—Donnerwetter, during breakfast and all along the road I conjugated until I saw green.——I must have popped off to sleep shortly after three. My pen made a blot in the book. The lamp was smoking when Mathilde woke me; the blackbirds in the elder bushes under the window were chirping so happily——and I felt so inexpressibly melancholy. I put on my collar and passed the brush through my hair.——One feels it when one imposes upon nature.

MELCHIOR.

May I roll you a cigarette?

MORITZ.

Thanks, I don't smoke.——If it only keeps on this way! I will work and work until my eyes fall out of my head.——Ernest Röbel has failed three times since vacation; three times in Greek, twice with Knochenbruch; the last time in the history of literature. I have been first five times in this lamentable conflict, and from to-day it does not bother me!——Röbel will not shoot himself. Röbel has no parents who sacrifice everything for him. If he wants he can become a soldier, a cowboy or a sailor. If I fail, my father will feel the blow and Mamma will land in the madhouse. One can't live through a thing like that!——Before the examination I

41

begged God to give me consumption that the cup might pass me by untouched. He passed me by, though to-day His aureole shines in the distance, so that I dare not lift my eyes by night or day.——Now that I have grasped the bar I shall swing up on it. The natural consequence will be that I shall break my neck if I fall.

MELCHIOR.

Life is a worthless commonplace. It wouldn't have been a bad idea if I had hanged myself in the cradle.——Why doesn't Mamma come with the tea!

MORITZ.

Your tea will do me good, Melchior!——I'm shivering. I feel so strangely spiritualized. Touch me once, please. I see,—I hear,—I feel, much more acutely——and yet everything seems like a dream——oh, so harmonious.——How still the garden stretches out there in the moon-light, so still, so deep, as if it extended to eternity. From out the bushes step indefinable figures that slip away in breathless officiousness through the clearings and then vanish in the twilight. It seems to me as if a coun-sel were to be held under the chestnut tree.——Shall we go down there, Melchior?

MELCHIOR.

Let's wait until we have drunk our tea.

MORITZ.

The leaves whisper so busily.——It's just as if I heard my dead grandmother telling me the story of the "Queen Without a Head." There was once a wonderfully beautiful Queen, beautiful as the sun, more beautiful than all the maidens in the country. Only, unfortunately, she came into the world without a head. She could not eat, not drink, not kiss. She could only communicate with her courtiers by using her soft little hand. With her dainty feet she stamped declarations of war and orders for executions. Then, one day, she was besieged by a King, who, by chance, had two heads, which, year in and year out, disputed with one another so violently that neither could get a word in edgewise. The Court Conjurer-in-chief took off the smallest of these heads and set it upon the Queen's body. And, behold, it became her extraordinarily well! Therefore, the King and the Queen were married, and the two heads disputed no longer, but kissed each other upon the brow, the cheeks and the mouth, and lived thereafter through long, long years of joy and peace.——Delectable nonsense! Since vacation I can't get the headless Queen out of my mind. When I see a pretty girl, I see her without a head——and then presently, I, myself appear to be the headless Queen.——It is possible that someone may be set over me yet.

(*Frau Gabor comes in with the steaming tea, which she sets before Melchior and Moritz on the table.*)

FRAU GABOR.

Here, children, here's a mouthful for you. Good-evening, Herr Stiefel, how are you?

MORITZ.

Thank you, Frau Gabor.——I'm watching the dance down there.

FRAU GABOR.

But you don't look very good——don't you feel well?

MORITZ.

It's not worth mentioning. I went to bed somewhat too late last night.

MELCHIOR.

Only think, he worked all through the night.

FRAU GABOR.

You shouldn't do such things, Herr Stiefel. You ought to take care of yourself. Think of your health. Don't set your school above your health. Take plenty of walks in the fresh air. At your age, that is more important than a correct use of middle high German.

MORITZ.

I will go walking. You are right. One can be industrious while one is taking a walk. Why didn't I think of that myself!——The written work I shall still have to do at home.

MELCHIOR.

You can do your writing here; that will make it easier for both of us.——
You know, Mamma, that Max von Trenk has been down with brain
fever!——To-day at noon Hans Rilow came from von Trenk's deathbed
to announce to Rector Sonnenstich that von Trenk had just died in his
presence. "Indeed?" said Sonnenstich, "haven't you two hours from last
week to make up? Here is the beadle's report. See that the matter is
cleared up once for all! The whole class will attend the burial."——Hans
was struck dumb.

FRAU GABOR.

What book is that you have, Melchior?

MELCHIOR.

"Faust."

FRAU GABOR.

Have you read it yet?

MELCHIOR.

Not to the end.

MORITZ.

We're just at the Walpurgisnacht.

FRAU GABOR.

If I were you I should have waited for one or two years.

MELCHIOR.

I know of no book, Mamma, in which I have found so much beauty. Why
shouldn't I read it?

FRAU GABOR.

Because you can't understand it.

MELCHIOR.

You can't know that, Mamma. I feel very well that I am not yet able to grasp the work in its entirety——

MORITZ.

We always read together; that helps our understanding wonderfully.

FRAU GABOR.

You are old enough, Melchior, to be able to know what is good and what is bad for you. Do what you think best for yourself. I should be the first to acknowledge your right in this respect, because you have never given me a reason to have to deny you anything. I only want to warn you that even the best can do one harm when one isn't ripe enough in years to receive it properly.——I would rather put my trust in you than in conventional educational methods.——If you need anything, children, you, Melchior, come up and call me. I shall be in my bedroom. (*Exit.*)

MORITZ.

Your Mamma means the story of Gretchen.

MELCHIOR.

Weren't we discussing it just a moment ago!

MORITZ.

Faust himself cannot have deserted her in cold blood!

MELCHIOR.

The masterpiece does not end with this infamous action!——Faust might have promised the maiden marriage, he might have forsaken her afterwards, but in my eyes he would have been not a hair less worthy of punishment. Gretchen might have died of a broken heart for all I care.——One sees how this attracts the eyes continually; one might think that the whole world turned on sex![2]

---

[2] "*Man möchte glauben, die ganze Welt drehe sich um P—— und V——!*"

45

MORITZ.

To be frank with you, Melchior, I have almost the same feeling since I read your explanation.——It fell at my feet during the first vacation days. I was startled. I fastened the door and flew through the flaming lines as a frightened owl flies through a burning wood——I believe I read most of it with my eyes shut. Your explanation brought up a host of dim recollections, which affected me as a song of his childhood affects a man on his deathbed when heard from the lips of another. I felt the most vehement pity over what you wrote about maidens. I shall never lose that sensation. Believe me, Melchior, to suffer a wrong is sweeter than to do a wrong. To be overcome by such a sweet wrong and still be blameless seems to me the fullness of earthly bliss.

MELCHIOR.

I don't want my bliss as alms!

MORITZ.

But why not?

MELCHIOR.

I don't want anything for which I don't have to fight!

MORITZ.

Is it enjoyable then, Melchior?——The maiden's enjoyment is as that of the holy gods. The maiden controls herself, thanks to her self-denial. She keeps herself free from every bitterness until the last moment, in order that she may see the heavens open over her in an instant. The maiden fears hell even at the moment that she perceives a blooming paradise. Her feeling is as pure as a mountain spring. The maiden holds a cup over which no earthly breath has blown as yet; a nectar chalice, the contents of which is spilled when it flames and flares.——The enjoyment that the man finds in that, I think, is insipid and flat.

MELCHIOR.

You can think what you like about it, but keep your thoughts to yourself——I don't like to think about it.

46

SCENE SECOND.

A Dwelling Room.

FRAU BERGMANN.

(*Enters by the center door. Her face is beaming. She is without a hat, wears a mantilla on her head and has a basket on her arm.*)
Wendla! Wendla!

WENDLA.

(*Appears in petticoats and corset in the doorway to the right.*)
What's the matter, Mother?

FRAU BERGMANN.

You are up already, child? Now, that is nice of you!

WENDLA.

You have been out already?

FRAU BERGMANN.

Get dressed quickly!——You must go down to Ina's at once. You must take her this basket!

WENDLA.

(*Dressing herself during the following conversation.*)
You have been to Ina's?—How is Ina?—Is she ever going to get better?

FRAU BERGMANN.

Only think, Wendla, last night the stork paid her a visit and brought her a little baby boy!

WENDLA.

A little boy?——A little boy!——Oh, that's lovely!——That's the cause of that tedious influenza!

47

FRAU BERGMANN.

A fine little boy!

WENDLA.

I must see him, Mother. That makes me an aunt for the third time——aunt to a little girl and two little boys!

FRAU BERGMANN.

And what little boys!——It always happens that way when one lives so near the church roof!——To-morrow will be just two years since she went up the steps in her mull gown.

WENDLA.

Were you there when he brought him?

FRAU BERGMANN.

He had just flown away again.——Won't you put on a rose?

WENDLA.

Why couldn't you have been a little earlier, Mother?

FRAU BERGMANN.

I almost believe he brought you something, too——a breastpin or something.

WENDLA.

It's really a shame!

FRAU BERGMANN.

But, I tell you, he brought you a breastpin!

WENDLA.

I have breastpins enough——

FRAU BERGMANN.

Then be happy, child. What do you want besides?

WENDLA.

I would have liked so much to have known whether he flew through the window or down the chimney.

FRAU BERGMANN.

You must ask Ina. Ha! You must ask Ina that, dear heart! Ina will tell you that fast enough. Ina talked with him for a whole half hour.

WENDLA.

I will ask Ina when I get there.

FRAU BERGMANN.

Now don't forget, sweet angel! I'm interested myself to know if he came in through the window or by the chimney.

WENDLA.

Or hadn't I better ask the chimney-sweep?——The chimney-sweep must know best whether he flew down the chimney or not.

FRAU BERGMANN.

Not the chimney-sweep, child; not the chimney-sweep. What does the chimney-sweep know about the stork! He'd tell you a lot of foolishness he didn't believe himself——Wha——what are you staring at down there in the street?

WENDLA.

A man, Mother,——three times as big as an ox!——with feet like steamboats ——!

FRAU BERGMANN.

(*Rushing to the window.*)
Impossible! Impossible!

WENDLA.

(*At the same time.*)
He holds a bedslat under his chin and fiddles "Die Wacht am Rhein" on it——there, he's just turned the corner.——

FRAU BERGMANN.

You are, and always will be a foolish child!——To frighten your old simple mother that way!——Go get your hat! I wonder when you will understand things. I've given up hope of you.

WENDLA.

So have I, Mother dear, so have I. It's a sad thing about my understanding.——I have a sister who has been married for two and a half years, I myself have been made an aunt for the third time, and I haven't the least idea how it all comes about.——Don't be cross, Mother dear, don't be cross! Whom in the world should I ask but you! Please tell me, dear Mother! Tell me, dear Mother! I'm ashamed for myself. Please, Mother, speak! Don't scold me for asking you about it. Give me an answer——How does it happen?——How does it all come about?——You cannot really deceive yourself that I, who am fourteen years old, still believe in the stork.

FRAU BERGMANN.

Good. Lord, child, but you are peculiar!——What ideas you have!——I really can't do that!

WENDLA.

But why not, Mother?——Why not?——It can't be anything ugly if everybody is delighted over it!

FRAU BERGMANN.

O——O God protect me!——I deserve——Go get dressed, child, go get dressed!

WENDLA.

I'll go——And suppose your child went and asked the chimney-sweep?

FRAU BERGMANN.

But that would be madness!——Come here, child, come here, I'll tell you!
I'll tell you everything——O Almighty Goodness!——only not to-day,
Wendla!——To-morrow, the next day, next week——any time you want,
dear heart——

WENDLA.

Tell me to-day, Mother; tell me now! Right away!——Now that I have seen
you so frightened I can never be peaceful until you do.

FRAU BERGMANN.

I can't do it, Wendla.

WENDLA.

Oh, why can't you, Mother dear!——I will kneel here at your feet and lay
my head in your lap. You can cover my head with your apron and talk
and talk, as if you were entirely alone in the room. I won't move, I won't
cry, I will bear all patiently, no matter what may come.

FRAU BERGMANN.

Heaven knows, Wendla, that I am not to blame! Heaven knows it!——
Come here in God's name! I will tell you, child, how you came into this
world.——Listen to me, Wendla.——

WENDLA.

(*Under the apron.*)
I'm listening.

FRAU BERGMANN.

(*Extatically.*)
But it's no use, child!——I can't justify it. I deserve to be put into prison—
—to have you taken from me.

WENDLA.

Take heart, Mother!

51

FRAU BERGMANN.

Listen, then——!

WENDLA.

(*Trembling under the apron.*)
O God! O God!

FRAU BERGMANN.

In order to have a child——do you understand me, Wendla?

WENDLA.

Quick, Mother, I can't stand it much longer.

FRAU BERGMANN.

In order to have a child——one must love—the man—to whom one is
married—love him, I tell you—as one can only love a man! One must
love him so much with one's whole heart, so—so that one can't describe
it! One must love him, Wendla, as you at your age are still unable to
love——Now you know it!

WENDLA.

(*Getting up.*)
Great——God——in heaven!

FRAU BERGMANN.

Now you know what an ordeal awaits you!

WENDLA.

And that is all?

FRAU BERGMANN.

As true as God helps me!——Take your basket now and go to Ina. You will
get chocolate and cakes there.——Come, let's look you over, the laced
shoes, the silk gloves, the sailor blouse, the rose in your hair—your
dress is really becoming much too short for you, Wendla!

WENDLA.

Did you get meat for lunch, Mother?

FRAU BERGMANN.

The Good God protect and bless you——I will find an opportunity to add
a handbreadth of flounces to the bottom.

SCENE THIRD.

HANS RILOW.

(*With a light in his hand, fastens the door behind him and opens the lid.*)
"Have you prayed to-night, Desdemona?" (*He takes a reproduction of the
Venus of Palma Vecchio from his bosom.*)——Thou wilt not appear to me
after the Our Father, darling,——as in that moment of anticipated bliss
when I saw thee contemplatively expectant of someone's coming, lying
in Jonathan Schlesinger's shop window——just as enticing as thou art
now, with these supple limbs, these softly arched hips, these plump,
youthful breasts.——Oh how intoxicated with joy the great master must
have been when his glance strayed over the fourteen-year-old original
stretched out upon the divan!

Wilt thou not visit me for awhile in my dreams? I will receive thee with
widely open arms and will kiss thee until thou art breathless. Thou
drawest me onward as the enchanted princess in her deserted castle.
Portals and doors open themselves as if by an unseen hand, while the
fountain in the park below begins to splash joyously——

"It is the cause!——It is the cause!" The frightful beating in my breast shows
thee that I do not murder thee from frivolous emotion. The thought of
my lonely nights is strangling me. I swear to thee, child, on my soul,
that it is not satiety which rules me. Who could ever boast of being
satiated of thee!

But thou suckest the marrow from my bones, thou bendest my back, thou
robbest my youthful eyes of their last spark of brilliancy.——Thou art
so arrogant toward me in thy inhuman modesty, so galling with thy
immovable limbs!——Thou or I! And I have won the victory.

Suppose I count them——all those who sleep, with whom I have fought
the same battle here——: Psyche by Thumann—another bequest from
the spindle-shanked Mademoiselle Angelique, that rattlesnake in the

paradise of my childhood; Io by Corregio; Galathea by Lossow; then a Cupid by Bouguereau; Ada by J. van Beers—that Ada whom I had to abduct from a secret drawer in Papa's secretary in order to incorporate in my harem; a trembling, modest Leda by Makart, whom I found by chance among my brother's college books——seven, thou blooming candidate for death, have preceded thee upon this path to Tartarus. Let that be a consolation unto thee, and seek not to increase my torments at this enormity by that fleeting look.

Thou diest not for thy sins, thou diest on account of mine!——As protection against myself I go to my seventh wife-murder with a bleeding heart. There is something tragic in the rôle of Bluebeard. I believe the combined sufferings of his murdered wives did not equal the torments he underwent each time he strangled one of them.

But my thoughts will become more peaceful, my body will strengthen itself, when thou, thou little devil, residest no longer in the red satin padding of my jewel case. In place of thee, I will indulge in wanton joyousness with Bodenhausen's Lurlei or Linger's Forsaken One, or Defregger's Loni—so I should be all the quicker! But a quarter of a year more, perhaps thy unveiled charms, sweet soul, would begin to consume my poor head as the sun does a pat of butter. It is high time to declare the divorce from bed and board.

Brrr! I feel a Heliogablus within me? Moritura me salutat! Maiden, maiden, why dost thou press thy knees together?——Why now of all times?—— In face of the inscrutable eternity?——A movement and I will spare thy life!——A womanly emotion, a sign of passion, of sympathy, maiden!— —I will frame thee in gold, and hang thee over my bed! Doest thou not guess that only thy chastity begets my debauchery?——Woe, woe, unto the inhuman ones!——

One always perceives that they received an exemplary education——It is just so with me.

"Have you prayed to-night, Desdemona?"

My heart contracts,——madness!——St. Agnes also died for her reserve and was not half as naked as thou!——Another kiss upon thy blooming body——upon thy childish swelling breast—upon thy sweetly rounded— thy cruel knees——

"It is the cause, it is the cause, my soul, Let me not name it to you, you chaste stars! It is the cause!"——

(*The picture falls into the depths, he shuts the lid.*)

FOURTH SCENE.

A haymow. Melchior lies on his back in the fresh hay. Wendla comes up the ladder.

WENDLA.

Here's where you've hid yourself?——They're all hunting for you. The wagon is outside again. You must help. There's a storm coming up.

MELCHIOR.

Go away from me! Go away from me!

WENDLA.

What's the matter with you?——Why are you hiding your face?

MELCHIOR.

Out! out! I'll throw you down on the floor below.

WENDLA.

Now for certain I'm not going.—(*Kneels down by him.*) Why won't you come out with me into the meadow, Melchior?——Here it is hot and dark. Suppose we do get wet to the skin, what difference will that make to us!

MELCHIOR.

The hay smells so fine.——The sky outside must be as black as a pall——I only see the brilliant poppy on your breast——and I hear your heart beating——

WENDLA.

Don't kiss me, Melchior!——Don't kiss me!

MELCHIOR.

Your heart——I hear beating——

WENDLA.

People love——when they kiss——Don't, don't!

MELCHIOR.

Oh, believe me, there's no such thing as love! Everything is selfishness, everything is egotism!——I love you as little as you love me.

WENDLA.

Don't——don't, Melchior!——

MELCHIOR.

Wendla.

WENDLA.

Oh, Melchior!——Don't, don't——

FIFTH SCENE.

FRAU GABOR.

(*Sits writing.*)

Dear Herr Stiefel:—After twenty-four hours of consideration and re-consideration of all you have written me, I take up my pen with a heavy heart. I cannot furnish you with the necessary amount for the voyage to America—I give you my word of honor. In the first place, I have not that much to my credit, and in the second place, if I had, it would be the greatest sin imaginable for me to put into your hands the means of accomplishing such an ill-considered measure. You will be doing me a bitter wrong, Herr Stiefel, if you see a sign of lack of love in my refusal. On the contrary, it would be the greatest neglect of my duty as your motherly friend were I to allow myself to be affected by your temporary lack of determination, so that I also lost my head and blindly followed my first fleeting impulse. I am very ready—in case you desire it—to write to your parents. I should seek to convince your parents that you have done what you could during this quarter, that you have exhausted your strength, that a rigorous judgment of your case would not only be inadvisable, but might be in the greatest degree prejudicial to your mental and bodily health.

That you imply a threat to take your own life in case flight is impossible for you, to speak plainly, has somewhat surprised me. No matter how undeserving is a misfortune, Herr Stiefel, one should never choose improper means to escape it. The way in which you, to whom I have always done only good, want to make me responsible for a possible frightful action on your part, has something about it which, in the eyes of an evil-thinking person, might be misconstrued very easily. I must confess that this outbreak of yours—you who know so well what one owes to oneself—is the last thing for which I was prepared. However, I cherish the strong conviction that you are laboring yet too much under the shock of your first fright to be able to understand completely your action.

And, therefore, I hope with confidence that these words of mine will find you already in better spirits. Take up the matter as it stands. In my opinion it is unwise to judge a young man by his school record. We have too many examples of bad students becoming distinguished men, and, on the other hand, of brilliant students not being at all remarkable in life. At any rate, I can assure you that your misfortune, as far as it lies with me, shall make no difference in your association with Melchior. On the contrary, it will afford me the greatest pleasure to see my son going with a young man who, let the world judge him as it will, is able to win my fullest sympathy.

And, therefore, hold your head high, Herr Stiefel!——Such a crisis as this comes to all of us and will soon be surmounted. If all of us had recourse to dagger or poison in such cases, there would soon be no men left in the world. Let me hear from you right soon again, and accept the heartfelt greetings of your unchanged

Motherly friend,
Fanny G.

SCENE SIXTH.

Bergmann's garden in the morning sunlight.

WENDLA.

Why have you slipped out of the room?——To hunt violets!——Because Mother seems to laugh at me.——Why can't you bring your lips together any more?——I don't know.——Indeed I don't know, I can't find words——The path is like a velvet carpet, no pebbles, no thorns.——My feet don't touch the ground.——Oh, how I slept last night!

Here they are.——I become as grave as a nun at communion.——Sweet violets!——Peace, little mother, I will put on my long dress.——Oh God, if somebody would come upon whose neck I could fall and tell!

SCENE SEVEN.

Evening twilight. Light clouds in the sky. The path straggles through low bushes and coarse grass. The flow of the stream is heard in the distance.

MORITZ.

Better and better.——I am not fit. Another may be able to climb to the top. I pull the door to behind me and step into the open.——I don't care enough about it to let myself be turned back.

I haven't succeeded in forcing my way. How shall I force my way now!——I have no contract with God. Let them make out of the thing what they will. I have been forced.——I do not hold my parents answerable. At the same time, the worst must fall upon them. They were old enough to know what they were doing. I was a weakling when I came into the world——or else I would have been wise enough to become another being. Why should I be forced to pay for the fact that the others were here already!

I must have fallen on my head——If anybody makes me a present of a mad dog I'll give him back a mad dog. And if he won't take back his mad dog, then I am human and——

I must have fallen on my head!

Man is born by chance and should not, after mature consideration——It is to shoot oneself dead!

The weather at least has shown itself considerate. The whole day it looked like rain and yet it has held off.——A rare peace rules in nature. Nowhere anything dazzling, exciting. Heaven and earth are like a transparent fabric. And everything seems so happy. The landscape is as sweet as the melody of a lullaby.——"Sleep, little prince, sleep on," as Fräulein Snandulia sang. It's a shame she holds her elbows so awkwardly!——I danced for the last time at the Cäcilienfest. Snandulia only dances with good matches.——Her silk dress was cut low in front and in the back. In the back, down to her girdle and in the front down——unconscionably low.——She couldn't have worn a chemise.———That might be something able to affect me yet.——More than half curiosity.——It must be a wonderful sensation——a feeling as if one were being carried through the rapids——I should never tell anybody that I was experiencing something untried before——I would act as if I had done it all.—There is something shameful in growing up to be a man without having learned the chief function of masculinity.——You come from Egypt, honorable sir, and have not seen the pyramids?!

I will not cry again to-day. I will not think of my burial again.——Melchior will lay a wreath on my coffin. Pastor Kahlbauch will console my parents. Rector Sonnenstich will cite examples from history.——It is possible that I shall not have a tombstone. I had wanted a snow-white marble urn on a pedestal of black syenite.——Thank God, I shall not miss them. Monuments are for the living, not for the dead.

I should need a whole year to say farewell to everything in my thoughts. I will not cry again. I am so happy to be able to look back without bitterness. How many beautiful evenings I have passed with Melchior!——under the osiers; at the forester's house; on the highway where the five lindens stand; on the Schlossberg, among the restful ruins of the Runenburg.——When the hour comes, I will think with all my might of whipped cream. Whipped cream doesn't stay firm. It falls and leaves a pleasant after-taste.——I had thought men were infinitely worse. I haven't found one who didn't want to do his best. Many have suffered with me on my own account.

I wander to the altar like the ancient Etrurian youth whose dying rattle bought his brothers' prosperity for the coming year.——I experience bit by bit the mysterious awe of liberation. I sob with sorrow over my lot.——Life has turned its cold shoulder to me. I see earnest, friendly glances luring me there in the distance, the headless queen, the headless queen—compassion awaiting me with open arms——Your commands concern minors; I carry my free ticket in myself. If the shell sinks, the butterfly flits from it; the delusion no longer holds.——You should drive no mad bargain with the swindle! The mists close in; life is bitter on the tongue.

ILSE.

(*In torn clothing, a bright cloth about her head, grabs him by the shoulder from behind.*)
What have you lost?

MORITZ.

Ilse!

ILSE.

What are you hunting here?

MORITZ.

Why did you frighten me so?

ILSE.

What are you hunting?——What have you lost?

MORITZ.

Why did you frighten me so fearfully?

ILSE.

I'm coming from town.——I'm going home.

MORITZ.

I don't know what I've lost.

ILSE.

Then seeking won't help you.

MORITZ.

Sakerment, sakerment!

ILSE.

I haven't been home for four days.

MORITZ.

Restless as a cat!

ILSE.

Because I have on my dancing slippers——Mother will make eyes!——
Come to our house with me!

MORITZ.

Where have you been strolling again?

ILSE.

With the Priapia!

MORITZ.

Priapia?

ILSE.

With Nohl, with Fehrendorf, with Padinsky, with Lenz, Rank, Spühler—
with all of them possible! Kling, kling——things were lively!

MORITZ.

Do they paint you?

ILSE.

Fehrendorf painted me as a pillar saint. I am standing on a Corinthian
capital. Fehrendorf, I tell you, is a gibbering idiot. The last time, I trod
on one of his tubes. He wiped his brush on my hair. I fetched him a
box on the ear. He threw his palette at my head. I upset the easel. He
chased me all about the studio, over divans, tables and chairs, with his
mahlstick. Behind the stove stood a sketch;——Be good or I'll tear it!
He swore amnesty, and—and then kissed me promptly and frightfully,
frightfully, I tell you.

MORITZ.

Where do you spend the night when you stop in town?

ILSE.

Yesterday we were at Nohl's.——The day before with Bojokewitsch—Sunday with Oikonomopulos. We had champagne at Padinsky's. Valabregez had sold his "Woman Dead of the Pest." Adolar drank out of the ash tray. Lenz sang the "Child's Murderer," and Adolar pounded the guitar out of shape. I was so drunk they had to put me to bed.——Do you go to school yet, Moritz?

MORITZ.

No, no,——I take my leave of it this quarter.

ILSE.

You are right. Ah, how time passes when one earns money!——Do you remember how we used to play robbers?——Wendla Bergmann and you and I and the others, when you used to come out in the evening and drink warm goat's milk at our house?——What is Wendla doing? I haven't seen her since the flood——What is Melchi Gabor doing?—— Does he seem as deep thinking as ever?——We used to stand opposite each other during singing.

MORITZ.

He philosophizes.

ILSE.

Wendla came to see us a while ago and brought Mother some presents. I sat that day for Isidor Landauer. He needed me for the Holy Mary, the Mother of God, with the Christ Child. He is a ninny and disagreeable. Hu, like a weathercock!——Have you a katzenjammer?

MORITZ.

From last night!——We soaked like hippopotami. I staggered home at five o'clock.

ILSE.

One need only to look at you.— —Were there any girls there?

MORITZ.

Arabella, the beer nymph, an Andalusian. The landlord let all of us spend the whole night alone with her.

ILSE.

One only need look at you, Moritz!— —I don't know what a katzenjammer's like. During the last carnival I went three days and three nights without going to bed or taking my clothes off. From the ball to the café, noon at Bellavista; evenings, Tingle-Tangle; night, to the ball. Lena was there, and the fat Viola.— —The third night Heinrich found me.

MORITZ.

Had he been looking for you?

ILSE.

He tripped over my arm. I lay senseless in the snow in the street.— —That's how I went with him. For fourteen days I didn't leave his lodgings— —a dreadful time! In the morning I had to throw on his Persian nightgown and in the evening go about the room in the black costume of a page; white lace ruffles at my neck, my knees and my wrists. Every day he photographed me in some new arrangement— —once on the sofa as Ariadne, once as Leda, once as Ganymede, once on all fours as a feminine Nebuchadnezzar. Then he longed for murder, for shooting, suicide and coal gas. Early in the morning he brought a pistol into bed, loaded it full of shot and put it against my breast! A twitch and I'll pull!— —Oh, he would have fired, Moritz, he would have fired!— —Then he put the thing in his mouth like a blow-pipe.— —That awoke the feeling of self-preservation. And then— —brrr!— —the shot might have gone through my spine.

MORITZ.

Is Heinrich living yet?

ILSE.

How do I know!——Over the bed was a large mirror set into the ceiling. The room seemed as high as a tower and as bright as an opera house. One saw one's self hanging down bodily from heaven. I had frightful dreams at night——O God, O God, if it were only day!——Good-night, Ilse, when you are asleep you will be pretty to murder!

MORITZ.

Is this Heinrich living yet?

ILSE.

Please God, no!——One day, when he went for absinthe, I put on the mantle and ran out into the street. The carnival was over; the police arrested me; what was I doing in man's clothes?——They took me to the Central Station. Nohl, Fehrendorf, Padinsky, Spühler, Oikonomopulos, the whole Priapia came there and bailed me out. They transported me in a cab to Adolar's studio. Since then I've been true to the herd. Fehrendorf is an ape, Nohl is a pig, Bojokewitsch an owl, Loison a hyena, Oikonomopulos a camel——therefore I love one and all of them the same and wouldn't attach myself to anyone else, even if the world were full of archangels and millionaires!

MORITZ.

I must go back, Ilse.

ILSE.

Come as far as our house with me!

MORITZ.

What for?——What for?——

ILSE.

To drink warm goat's milk! I will singe your hair and hang a little bell around your neck.——Then we have another kid with which you can play.

MORITZ.

I must go back. I have yet the Sassanides, the Sermon on the Mount and the parallelepipedon on my thoughts.——Good-night, Ilse!

ILSE.

Sleep well!——Do you ever go to the wigwam where Melchi Gabor buried my tomahawk?——Brrr! until you are married I'll lie in the straw. (*Runs out.*)

MORITZ.

(*Alone.*)

It might have cost only a word.——(*He calls*)——Ilse?——Ilse!——Thank God she doesn't hear me any more.——I am not in the humor.——One needs a clear head and a happy heart for it.——What a lost opportunity!——I would have said that I had many crystal mirrors over my bed——that I had trained an unbroken filly——that I had her proudly march in front of me on the carpet in long black silk stockings and black patent leather shoes, long black gloves, black velvet about her neck——had strangled her in a moment of madness with my cushions. I would laugh when the talk turned on passion——I would cry out!——Cry out!——Cry out! It is you, Ilse!——Priapia!——Loss of memory!——That takes my strength!——This child of fortune, this sunny child——this joyous maiden on my dolorous path!——O!——O!——— —— —— —— —— —— —— —— ——
—— —— —— —— —— —— —— —— —— —— ——

(*In the bushes by the bank.*)

Have I found it again unwillingly—the seat of turf. The mulleins seem to have grown since yesterday. The outlook between the willows is still the same——The water runs as heavy as melted lead. I mustn't forget. (*He takes Frau Gabor's letter from his pocket and burns it.*)——How the sparks fly—here and there, downward and upward——souls!—— shooting stars!

Before I struck a light one could see the grass and a streak on the horizon.——Now it is dark. Now I shall never return home again.

ACT III

SCENE FIRST.

The Board Room—On the walls pictures of Pestalozzi and Jean Jacques Rousseau.

Professors Affenschmalz, Knüppeldick, Hungergurt, Knochenbruch, Zungenschlag and Fliegentod are seated around a green-covered table, over which are burning several gas jets. At the upper end, on a raised seat, is Rector Sonnenstich. Beadle Habebald squats near the door.

SONNENSTICH.

Has any gentleman something further to remark?——Gentlemen! We cannot help moving the expulsion of our guilty pupil before the National Board of Education; there are the strongest reasons why we cannot: We cannot, because we must expiate the misfortune which has fallen upon us already; we cannot, because of our need to protect ourselves from similar blows in the future; we cannot, because we must chastise our guilty pupil for the demoralizing influence he exerted upon his classmates; we cannot, above all, because we must hinder him from exerting the same influence upon his remaining classmates. We cannot ignore the charge—and this, gentlemen, is possibly the weightiest of all——on any pretext concerning a ruined career, because it is our duty to protect ourselves from an epidemic of suicide similar to that which has broken out recently in various grammar schools, and which until to-day has mocked all attempts of the teachers to shackle it by any means known to advanced education——Has any gentleman something further to remark?

KNÜPPELDICK.

I can rid myself of the conception no longer that it is time at last to open a window here.

66

ZUNGENSCHLAG.

Th- th- there is an a- a- at- atmosphere here li- li- like th- th- that of the cata- catacombs, like that in the document room of the former Cha-Cha-Chamber of Justice at Wetzlar.

SONNENSTICH.

Habebald!

HABEBALD.

At your service, Herr Rector.

SONNENSTICH.

Open a window. Thank God there's fresh air enough outside.——Has any other gentleman anything to say?

FLIEGENTOD.

If my associate wants to have a window opened, I haven't the least objection to it. Only I should like to ask that the window opened is not the one directly behind my back!

SONNENSTICH.

Habebald!

HABEBALD.

At your service, Herr Rector.

SONNENSTICH.

Open the other window!——Has any other gentleman anything to remark?

HUNGERGURT.

Without wishing to increase the controversy, I should like to recall the important fact that the other window has been walled up since vacation.

SONNENSTICH.

Habebald!

HABEBALD.

At your service, Herr Rector.

SONNENSTICH.

Leave the other window shut!——I find it necessary, gentlemen, to put this matter to a vote. I request those who are in favor of having the only window which can enter into this discussion opened to rise from their seats. (*He counts.*) One, two, three——one, two, three——Habebald!

HABEBALD.

At your service, Herr Rector.

SONNENSTICH.

Leave that window shut likewise! I, for my part, am of the opinion that the air here leaves nothing to be desired!——Has any gentleman anything further to remark?——Let us suppose that we omitted to move the expulsion of our guilty pupil before the National Board of Education, then the National Board of Education would hold us responsible for the misfortune which has overwhelmed us. Of the various grammar schools visited by the epidemic of self-murder, those in which the devastation of self-murder has reached 25 per cent. have been closed by the National Board of Education. It is our duty, as the guardians and protectors of our institute, to protect our institute from this staggering blow. It grieves us deeply, gentlemen, that we are not in a position to consider the other qualifications of our guilt-laden pupil as mitigating circumstances. An indulgent treatment, which would allow our guilty pupil to be vindicated, would not in any conceivable way imaginable vindicate the present imperiled existence of our institute. We see ourselves under the necessity of judging the guilt-laden that we may not be judged guilty ourselves.——Habebald!

HABEBALD.

At your service, Herr Rector!

SONNENSTICH.

Bring him up! (*Exit Habebald.*)

Zungenschlag.

If the pre-present atmosphere leaves little or nothing to desire, I should like to suggest that the other window be walled up during the summer va- va- va- vacation.

Fliegentod.

If our esteemed colleague, Zungenschlag, does not find our room ventilated sufficiently, I should like to suggest that our esteemed colleague, Zungenschlag, have a ventilator set into his forehead.

Zungenschlag.

I do- do- don't have to stand that!——I- I- I- I- do- do- don't have to st- st- st- stand rudeness!——I have my fi- fi- five senses!

Sonnenstich.

I must ask our esteemed colleagues, Fliegentod and Zungenschlag, to preserve decorum. It seems to me that our guilt-laden pupil is already on the stairs.
(*Habebald opens the door, whereupon Melchior, pale but collected, appears before the meeting.*)

Sonnenstich.

Come nearer to the table!——After Herr Stiefel became aware of the profligate deed of his son, the distracted father searched the remaining effects of his son Moritz, hoping if possible, to find the cause of the abominable deed, and discovered among them, in an unexpected place, a manuscript, which, while it did not make us understand the abominable deed, threw an unfortunate and sufficient light upon the moral disorder of the criminal. This manuscript, in the form of a dialogue entitled "The Nuptial Sleep," illustrated with life-size pictures full of shameless obscenity, has twenty pages of long explanations that seek to satisfy every claim a profligate imagination can make upon a lewd book.——

Melchior.

I have——

SONNENSTICH.

You have to keep quiet!——After Herr Stiefel had questioningly handed us this manuscript and we had promised the distracted father to discover the author at any price, we compared the handwriting before us with the collected handwriting of the fellow-students of the deceased profligate, and concluded, in the unanimous judgment of the teaching staff, as well as with the full coincidence of a valued colleague, the master of calligraphy, that the resemblance to your——

MELCHIOR.

I have——

SONNENSTICH.

You have to keep quiet!——In spite of this likeness, recognized as crushing evidence by incontrovertible authority, we believe that we should allow ourselves to go further and to take the widest latitude in examining the guilty one at first hand, in order to make him answerable to this charge of an offense against morals, and to discover its relationship to the resultant suicide.——

MELCHIOR.

I have——

SONNENSTICH.

You have to answer the exact questions which I shall put to you, one after the other, with a plain and modest "yes" or "no."——Habebald!

HABEBALD.

At your service, Herr Rector!

SONNENSTICH.

The minutes!——I request our writing master, Herr Fliegentod, from now on to take down the proceedings as nearly verbatim as possible.——(*to Melchior.*) Do you know this writing?

MELCHIOR.

Yes.

SONNENSTICH.

Do you know whose writing it is?

MELCHIOR.

Yes.

SONNENSTICH.

Is the writing in this manuscript yours?

MELCHIOR.

Yes.

SONNENSTICH.

Are you the author of this obscene manuscript?

MELCHIOR.

Yes——I request you, sir, to show me anything obscene in it.

SONNENSTICH.

You have to answer with a modest "yes" or "no" the exact questions which
I put to you!

MELCHIOR.

I have written neither more nor less than what are well-known facts to all
of you.

SONNENSTICH.

You shameless boy!

MELCHIOR.

I request you to show me an offense against morals in this manuscript!

SONNENSTICH.

Are you counting on a desire on my part to be a clown for you?——
Habebald——!

MELCHIOR.

I have——

SONNENSTICH.

You have as little respect for the dignity of your assembled teachers as you have a proper appreciation of mankind's innate sense of shame which belongs to a moral world!——Habebald!

HABEBALD.

At your service, Herr Rector!

SONNENSTICH.

It is past the time for the three hours' exercise in agglutive Volapuk.

MELCHIOR.

I have——

SONNENSTICH.

I will request our secretary, Herr Fliegentod, to close the minutes.

MELCHIOR.

I have——

SONNENSTICH.

You have to keep still!!——Habebald!

HABEBALD.

At your service, Herr Rector!

SONNENSTICH.

Take him down!

SCENE SECOND.

A graveyard in the pouring rain——Pastor Kahlbauch stands beside an open grave with a raised umbrella in his hand. To his right are Renter Stiefel, his friend Ziegenmelker and Uncle Probst. To the left Rector Sonnenstich with Professor Knochenbruch, The grammar school students complete the circle. Martha and Ilse stand somewhat apart upon a fallen monument.

PASTOR KAHLBAUCH.

For, he who rejects the grace with which the Everlasting Father has blessed those born in sin, he shall die a spiritual death!——He, however, who in willful carnal abnegation of God's proper honor, lives for and serves evil, shall die the death of the body!——Who, however, wickedly throws away from him the cross which the All Merciful has laid upon him for his sins, verily, verily, I say unto you, he shall die the everlasting death! (*He throws a shovelful of earth into the grave.*)——Let us, however, praise the All Gracious Lord and thank Him for His inscrutable grace in order that we may travel the thorny path more and more surely. For as truly as this one died a triple death, as truly will the Lord God conduct the righteous unto happiness and everlasting life.

RENTER STIEFEL.

(*His voice stopped with tears, throws a shovelful of earth into the grave.*)
The boy was nothing to me!——The boy was nothing to me!——The boy was a burden from his birth!

RECTOR SONNENSTICH.

(*Throws a shovelful of earth into the grave.*)
Suicide being the greatest conceivable fault against the moral order of the world, is the greatest evidence of the moral order of the world. The suicide himself spares the world the need of pronouncing judgment of condemnation against himself, and confirms the existence of the moral order of the world.

73

PROFESSOR KNOCHENBRUCH.

(*Throws a shovelful of earth into the grave.*)
Wasted—soiled—debauched—tattered and squandered!

UNCLE PROBST.

(*Throws a shovelful of earth into the grave.*)
I would not have believed my own mother had she told me that a child could act so basely towards its own parents.

FRIEND ZIEGENMELKER.

(*Throws a shovelful of earth into the grave.*)
To treat a father so, who for twenty years, from late to early, had no other thought than the welfare of his child!

PASTOR KAHLBAUCH.

(*Shaking Renter Stiefel's hand.*)
We know that those who love God serve all things best (1 Corinthians 12:15).——Think of the bereaved mother and strive to console her for her loss by doubled love.

RECTOR SONNENSTICH.

(*Shaking Renter Stiefel's hand.*)
Indeed, we could not possibly have promoted him.

PROFESSOR KNOCHENBRUCH.

(*Shaking Renter Stiefel's hand.*)
And if we had promoted him, next spring he would have certainly failed to pass.

UNCLE PROBST.

(*Shaking Renter Stiefel's hand.*)
It is your duty now to think of yourself first of all. You are the father of a family——

FRIEND ZIEGENMELKER.

(*Shaking Renter Stiefel's hand.*)

Trust yourself to my guidance!——This devilish weather shakes one's guts!——The man who doesn't prevent it with a grog will ruin his heart valves.

RENTER STIEFEL.

(*Blowing his nose.*)

The boy was nothing to me——the boy was nothing to me!

(*Renter Stiefel leaves, accompanied by Pastor Kahlbauch, Rector Sonnenstich, Professor Knockenbruch, Uncle Probst and Friend Ziegenmelker.——The rain ceases.*)

HANS RILOW.

(*Throws a shovelful of earth into the grave.*)

Rest in peace, you honest fellow!——Greet my eternal brides for me, those sacrificed remembrances, and commend me respectfully to the grace of God——you poor clown——They will put a scarecrow on top of your grave because of your angelic simplicity.

GEORGE.

Did they find the pistol?

ROBERT.

There's no use looking for the pistol!

ERNEST.

Did you see him, Robert?

ROBERT.

It's a damned infernal swindle!——Who did see him?——Who did?

OTTO.

He was hidden!——They threw a covering over him.

75

GEORGE.

Was his tongue hanging out?

ROBERT.

His eyes——That's why they threw the cloth over him.

OTTO.

Frightful!

HANS RILOW.

Do you know for certain that he hanged himself?

ERNEST.

They say he has no head left.

OTTO.

Incredible!——Nonsense!

ROBERT.

I have the clue in my hands. I have never seen a man who hanged himself that they haven't thrown a cloth over.

GEORGE.

He couldn't have taken his leave in a vulgarer way!

HANS RILOW.

The devil! Hanging is pretty enough!

OTTO.

He owes me five marks. We had a bet. He swore he would keep his place.

HANS RILOW.

You are to blame for his lying there. You called him a boaster.

OTTO.

Nonsense! I, too, must grind away all night. If he had learned the history of Greek literature he would not have had to hang himself!

ERNEST.

Have you your composition, Otto?

OTTO.

First comes the introduction.

ERNEST.

I don't know at all what to write.

GEORGE.

Weren't you there when Affenschmalz gave us the theme?

HANS RILOW.

I'll fake up something out of Democritus.

ERNST.

I will see if there is anything left to be found in Meyer's Little Encyclopedia.

OTTO.

Have you your Virgil for to-morrow?——
(*The schoolboys leave——Martha and Ilse approach the grave.*)

ILSE.

Quick, quick!——Here are the grave-diggers coming!

MARTHA.

Hadn't we better wait, Ilse?

ILSE.

What for?——We'll bring fresh ones. Always fresh ones. There are enough growing.

MARTHA.

You're right, Ilse!——(*She throws a wreath of ivy into the grave, Ilse drops her apron and allows a shower of fresh anemones to rain down on the coffin.*)

MARTHA.

I'll dig up our roses. I'll be beaten for it!——They will be of some use here.

ILSE.

I'll water them as often as I pass here. I'll fetch violets from the brook and bring some iris from our house.

MARTHA.

It will be beautiful!——beautiful!

ILSE.

I was just across the brook on that side when I heard the shot.

MARTHA.

Poor dear!

ILSE.

And I know the reason, too, Martha.

MARTHA.

Did he tell you anything?

ILSE.

Parallelepipedon! But don't tell anybody.

MARTHA.

My hand on it.

ILSE.

Here is the pistol.

MARTHA.

That's the reason they didn't find it!

ILSE.

I took it right out of his hand when I came along in the morning.

MARTHA.

Give it to me, Ilse!——Please give it to me!

ILSE.

No, I'm going to keep it for a souvenir.

MARTHA.

Is it true, Ilse, that he lay there without a head?

ILSE.

He must have loaded it with water!——The mulleins were spattered all over with blood. His brains were scattered about the pasture.

SCENE THIRD.

Herr and Frau Gabor.

FRAU GABOR.

They needed a scapegoat. They did not dare meet the charge that was made everywhere against themselves. And now that my child has had the misfortune to run his head into the noose at the right moment, shall I, his own mother, help to end the work of his executioners?——God keep me from it!

HERR GABOR.

For fourteen years I have looked on at your spirited educational methods in silence. They were contrary to my ideas. I had always lived in the conviction that a child was not a plaything; a child should have a claim upon our most earnest efforts. But, I said to myself, if the spirit and the grace of the one parent are able to compensate for the serious maxims of the other, they may be given preference over the serious maxims.——I am not reproaching you, Fanny, but don't stand in my way when I seek to right your injustice and mine toward the lad.

FRAU GABOR.

I will block the way for you as long as a warm drop of blood beats in me. My child would be lost in the House of Correction. A criminal nature might be bettered in such an institution. I don't know. A fine natured man would just as surely turn into a criminal, like the plants when they are kept from sun and light. I am conscious of no injustice on my part. To-day, as always, I thank heaven that it showed me the way to awaken righteousness of character and nobility of thought in my child. What has he done which is so frightful? It doesn't occur to me to apologize for him——now that they have hunted him out of school, he bears no fault! And if it was his fault he has paid for it. You may know better. You may be entirely right theoretically. But I cannot allow my only child to be forcibly hunted to death.

HERR GABOR.

That doesn't depend on us, Fanny. That is the risk we took with our happiness. He who is too weak to march stops by the wayside. And, in the end, it is not the worst when what was certain to come comes in time to be bettered. Heaven protect us from that! It is our duty to strengthen the loiterer as long as reason supplies a means.——That they have hunted him out of school is not his own fault. If they hadn't hunted him out of school, that wouldn't have been his fault, either!——You are so lighthearted. You perceive inconsiderable trifles when the question concerns a fundamental injury to character. You women are not accustomed to judge such things. Anyone who can write what Melchior wrote must be rotten to the core of his being. The mark is plain. A half-healthy nature wouldn't do such a thing. None of us are saints. Each of us wanders from the straight path. His writing, on the contrary, tramples on principle. His writing is no evidence of a chance slip in the usual way; it sets forth with dreadful plainness and a frankly definite purpose that natural longing, that propensity for immorality, because it is immorality. His writing manifests that exceptional state of spiritual corruption which we jurists classify under the term "moral imbecility."——If anything can be done in his case, I am not able to say. If we want to preserve a glimmer of hope, and keep our spotless consciences as the parents of the victim, it is time for us to go to work determinedly in earnest.—Don't let us contend any more, Fanny! I feel how hard it is for you. I know that you idolize him because he expresses so entirely your genial nature. Be stronger than yourself. Show yourself for once devoid of self-interest towards your son.

FRAU GABOR.

God help me, how can one get along that way! One must be a man to be able to talk that way! One must be a man to be able to blind oneself so with the dead letter! One must be a man to be so blind that one can't see what stares him in the eyes. I have conscientiously and thoughtfully managed Melchior from his first day, because I found him impressionable to his surroundings. Are we answerable for what has happened? A tile might fall off the roof upon your head to-morrow, and then comes your friend—your father, and, instead of taking care of you, tramples upon you!——I will not let my child be destroyed before my eyes. That's the reason I'm his mother.——It is inconceivable! It is not to be believed! What did he write, then, after all! Isn't it the most striking proof of his harmlessness, of his stupidity, of his childish obscurity, that he can write so!——One must possess no intuitive knowledge of mankind——one must be an out and out bureaucrat, or weak in intellect, to scent moral corruption here!——Say what you will. If you land Melchior in the House of Correction, I will get a divorce. Then let me see if I can't find help and means somewhere in the world to rescue my child from destruction.

HERR GABOR.

You must prepare yourself for it——if not to-day, then to-morrow. It is not easy for anyone to discount misfortune. I will stand beside you, and when your courage begins to fail will spare no trouble or effort to relieve your heart. The future seems so gray to me, so full of clouds——it only remains for you to leave me too.

FRAU GABOR.

I should never see him again: I should never see him again! He can't bear the vulgar. He will not be able to stand the dirt. He will break under restraint; the most frightful examples will be before his eyes!——And if I see him again——O, God, O, God, that joyous heart——his clear laughter——all, all,——his childish resolution to fight courageously for good and righteousness——oh, this morning sky, how I cherished it light and pure in his soul as my highest good——Hold me to account if the sin cries for expiation! Hold me to account! Do with me what you will! I will bear the guilt.——But keep your frightful hand off the boy.

HERR GABOR.

He has gone wrong!

FRAU GABOR.

He has not gone wrong!

HERR GABOR.

He has gone wrong!——I would have given everything to be able to spare your boundless love.——A terrified woman came to me this morning, scarcely able to control her speech, with this letter in her hand——a letter to her fifteen-year-old daughter. She had opened it simply out of curiosity; the girl was not at home.——In the letter Melchior explains to the fifteen-year-old girl that his manner of acting left him no peace, that he had sinned against her, etc., etc., and that naturally he would answer for it. She must not fret herself even if she felt results. He was already on the road after help; his expulsion made it easier for him. The previous false step could still lead to her happiness——and more of such irrational nonsense.

FRAU GABOR.

Impossible!

HERR GABOR.

The letter is forged. It's a cheat. Somebody is trying to take advantage of his generally known expulsion. I have not yet spoken to the lad about it——but please look at this hand! See the writing!

FRAU GABOR.

An unprecedented, shameless bit of knavery!

HERR GABOR.

That's what I'm afraid!

FRAU GABOR.

No, no——never, never!

HERR GABOR.

It would be so much the better for us.——The woman, wringing her hands, asked me what she should do. I told her she should not leave her fifteen-year-old daughter lying about a haymow. Fortunately she left me the letter.——If we send Melchior to another grammar school, where he is not under parental supervision, in three weeks we shall have the same result.——A new expulsion——his joyful heart will get used to it after awhile.——Tell me, Fanny, where shall I send the lad?

FRAU GABOR.

To the House of Correction——

HERR GABOR.

To the?——

FRAU GABOR.

House of Correction!

HERR GABOR.

He will find there, in the first place, that which has been wrongfully withheld from him at home, parental discipline, principles, and a moral constraint to which he must submit under all circumstances.——Moreover, the House of Correction is not a place of terror, as you think it. The greatest weight is laid in the establishment upon the development of Christian thought and sensibility. The lad will learn at last to follow good in place of desire and not to follow his natural instincts, but to observe the letter of the law.——A half hour ago I received a telegram from my brother that confirms the woman's statement. Melchior has confided in him and begged him for 200 marks in order to fly to England——

FRAU GABOR.

(*Covering her face.*)
Merciful heavens!

SCENE FOURTH.

The House of Correction.—A corridor.—Diethelm, Rheinhold, Ruprecht, Helmuth, Gaston and Melchior.

DIETHELM.

Here is a twenty pfennig piece!

RHEINHOLD.

What shall we do with it?

DIETHELM.

I will lay it on the floor. Arrange yourselves about it. Who can get it can keep it.

RUPRECHT.

Won't you join us, Melchior?

MELCHIOR.

No, thank you.

HELMUTH.

The Joseph!

GASTON.

He can't do anything else. He is here for recreation.

MELCHIOR.

(To himself.)

It is not wise for me to separate myself from them. They all have an eye on me. I must join them——or the creature goes to the devil—— imprisonment drives it to suicide.——If I break my neck, all is well!—— If I escape, that is good, too! I can only win. Ruprecht would become my friend. He has acquaintances here.——I had better give him the chapter of Judas' daughter-in-law, Thamar, of Moab, of Lot and his kindred, of Queen Vashti and of Abishag the Shunammite.——He has he unhappiest physiognomy of the lot of them.

RUPRECHT.

I have it!

HELMUTH.

I'll get it yet!

GASTON.

The day after to-morrow, perhaps.

HELMUTH.

Right away!——Now!——O God! O God!——

ALL.

Summa——Summa cum laude!!

RUPRECHT.

(*Taking the money.*)
Many thanks!

HELMUTH.

Here, you dog!

RUPRECHT.

You swine!

HELMUTH.

Gallows bird!

RUPRECHT.

(*Hits him in the face.*)
There! (*Runs away.*)

HELMUTH.

(*Running after him.*)
I'll strike you dead!

THE REST OF THEM.

(*Running after.*)
Chase him! Chase him! Chase him! Chase him!

MELCHIOR.

(*Alone, wandering toward the window.*)
The lightning rod runs down there.——One would have to wind a pocket
    handkerchief about it.——When I think of them the blood always rushes
    to my head. And Moritz turns my feet to lead.——I'll go to a newspaper.
    If they pay me by space I'll be a free lance!——collect the news of the
    day——write——locals——ethical——psychophysical——one doesn't
    starve so easily nowadays. Public soup houses, Café Temperance——
    The house is sixty feet high and the cornice is crumbling——They hate
    me——they hate me because I rob them of liberty. Handle myself as I
    will, there remain misdemeanors——I dare only hope in the course of
    the year, gradually——It will be new moon in eight days. To-morrow
    I'll grease the hinges. By Sunday evening I must find out somehow who
    has the key.——Sunday evening, during prayers, a cataleptic fit——I
    hope to God nobody else will be sick!——Everything seems as clear to
    me as if it had happened. Over the window-frames I can reach easily—a
    swing—a clutch—but one must wind a handkerchief about it.——There
    comes the head inquisitor. (*Exit to the left.*)
(*Dr. Prokrustes enters from the right with a locksmith.*)

DR. PROKRUSTES.

The window is on the third floor and has stinging nettles planted under it,
    but what do the degenerates care for stinging nettles!——Last winter
    one of them got out of the trap door on the roof, and we had the
    whole trouble of capturing him, bringing him back, and locking him
    up again——

THE LOCKSMITH.

Do you want the grating of wrought iron?

DR. PROKRUSTES.

Of wrought iron——riveted so they cannot meddle with it.

SCENE FIFTH.

A bedchamber.—Frau Bergmann, Ina Müller and Doctor von Brausepulver. Wendla, in bed.

DR. VON BRAUSEPULVER.

How old are you, exactly?

WENDLA.

Fourteen and a half.

DR. VON BRAUSEPULVER.

I have been ordering Blaud's pills for fifteen years and have noticed astonishing results in the majority of cases. I prefer them to cod liver oil and wine of iron. Begin with three or four pills a day, and increase the number just as soon as you are able. I ordered Fräulein Elfriede, Baroness von Witzleben to increase the number of them by one, every third day. The Baroness misunderstood me and increased the number every day by three. Scarcely three weeks later the Baroness was able to go to Pyrmont with her mother to complete her cure.——I will allow you to dispense with exhausting walks and extra meals; therefore, promise me, dear child, to take frequent exercise and to avoid unwholesome food as soon as the desire for it appears again. Then this palpitation of the heart will soon cease——and the headache, the chills, the giddiness——and this frightful indigestion. Fräulein Elfriede, Baroness von Witzleben, ate a whole roast chicken with new potatoes for her breakfast eight days after her convalescence.

FRAU BERGMANN.

May I offer you a glass of wine, Doctor?

DR. VON BRAUSEPULVER.

I thank you, dear Frau Bergmann, my carriage is waiting.——Do not take it so to heart. In a few weeks our dear little patient will be again as fresh and bright as a gazelle. Be of good cheer.——Good-day, Frau Bergmann, good-day, dear child, good-day, ladies——good-day.

(Frau Bergmann accompanies him to the door.)

INA.

(*At the window.*)

Now your plantains are in bloom again.——Can you see that from your bed?——A short display, hardly worth rejoicing over them, they come and go so quickly. I, too, must go right away now. Müller is waiting for me in front of the post-office, and I must go first to the dressmaker's. Mucki is to have his first trousers and Karl is to have new knit leggings for winter.

WENDLA.

Sometimes I feel so happy——all joy and sunshine. I had not guessed that it could go so well in one's heart! I want to go out, to go over the meadows in the twilight, to look for primroses along the river and to sit down on the banks and dream—Then comes the toothache, and I feel as if I had to die the next morning at daybreak; I grow hot and cold, it becomes dark before my eyes; and then the beast flutters inside.——As often as I wake up, I see Mother crying. Oh, that hurts me so.——I can't tell you how much, Ina!

INA.

Shall I lift your pillows higher?

FRAU BERGMANN.

(*Returning.*)

He thinks the vomiting will soon cease; and then you can get up in peace—
—I, too, think it would be better if you got up soon, Wendla.

INA.

Possibly when I visit you the next time you will be dancing around the house again. Good-bye, Mother. I must positively go to the dress-maker's. God guard you, Wendla dear. (*Kisses her.*) A speedy, speedy recovery! (*Exit Ina.*)

WENDLA.

What did he tell you, Mother, when he was outside?

FRAU BERGMANN.

He didn't say anything.——He said Fraülein von Witzleben was subject to fainting spells also. It is almost always so with chlorosis.

WENDLA.

Did he say that I have chlorosis, Mother?

FRAU BERGMANN.

You are to drink milk and eat meat and vegetables when your appetite comes back.

WENDLA.

O, Mother, Mother, I believe I haven't chlorosis——

FRAU BERGMANN.

You have chlorosis, child. Be calm, Wendla, be calm, you have chlorosis.

WENDLA.

No, Mother, no! I know it. I feel it. I haven't chlorosis. I have dropsy——

FRAU BERGMANN.

You have chlorosis. He said positively that you have chlorosis. Calm yourself, girl. You will get better.

WENDLA.

I won't get better. I have the dropsy, I must die, Mother.——O, Mother, I must die!

FRAU BERGMANN.

You must not die, child! You must not die—Great heavens, you must not die!

WENDLA.

But why do you weep so frightfully, then?

FRAU BERGMANN.

You must not die, child! You haven't the dropsy, you have a child, girl! You have a child!——Oh, why did you do that to me!

WENDLA.

I haven't done anything to you.

FRAU BERGMANN.

Oh don't deny it any more, Wendla!——I know everything. See, I didn't want to say a word to you.——Wendla, my Wendla——!

WENDLA.

But it's not possible, Mother. I'm not married yet!

FRAU BERGMANN.

Great Almighty God——that's just it, that you are not married! That is the most frightful thing of all!——Wendla, Wendla, Wendla, what have you done!!

WENDLA.

God knows, I don't know any more! We lay in the hay——I have loved nobody in the world as I do you, Mother.

FRAU BERGMANN.

My sweetheart——

WENDLA.

O Mother, why didn't you tell me everything!

FRAU BERGMANN.

Child, child, let us not make each other's hearts any heavier! Take hold of yourself! Don't make me desperate, child. To tell *that* to a fourteen-year-old girl! See, I expected that about as much as I did the sun going out. I haven't acted any differently towards you than my dear, good mother did toward me.——Oh, let us trust in the dear God, Wendla; let us hope for compassion, and have compassion toward ourselves! See, nothing has happened yet, child. And if we are not cowardly now, God won't forsake us.——Be cheerful, Wendla, be cheerful!——One sits so at the window with one's hands in one's lap, while everything changes to good, and then one realizes that one almost wanted to break one's heart——Wa——why are you shivering?

WENDLA.

Somebody knocked.

FRAU BERGMANN.

I didn't hear anything, dear heart. (*Goes and opens the door.*)

WENDLA.

But I heard it very plainly——Who is outside?

FRAU BERGMANN.

Nobody——Schmidt's Mother from Garden street.——You come just at the right time, Mother Schmidt.

SCENE SIXTH.

Men and women wine-dressers in the vineyard. The sun is setting behind the peaks of the mountains in the west. A clear sound of bells rises from the valley below. Hans Rilow and Ernest Röbel roll about in the dry grass of the highest plot under the overhanging rocks.

ERNEST.

I have overworked myself.

HANS.

Don't let us be sad!——It's a pity the minutes are passing.

ERNEST.

One sees them hanging and can't manage any more——and to-morrow they are in the wine press.

HANS.

Fatigue is as intolerable to me as hunger.

ERNEST.

Oh, I can't eat any more.

HANS.

Just this shining muscatelle!

ERNEST.

My elasticity has its limit.

HANS.

If I bend down the vine, we can sway it from mouth to mouth. Neither of us will have to disturb himself. We can bite off the grapes and let the branches fly back to the trunk.

ERNEST.

One hardly decides upon a thing, when, see, that vanishing power begins to darken.

HANS.

Hence the flaming firmament——and the evening bells——I promise myself little more for the future.

ERNEST.

Sometimes I see myself already as a worthy pastor—with a good-natured little wife, a well-filled library and offices and dignities all about me. For six days one has to think, and on the seventh one opens one's mouth. When out walking, one gives one's hand to the school-girls and boys, and when one comes home the coffee steams, the cookies are brought out and the maids fetch apples through the garden door.——Can you imagine anything more beautiful?

HANS.

I imagine half-closed eyelids, half-open lips and Turkish draperies.——I do not believe in pathos. Our elders show us long faces in order to hide their stupidity. Among themselves they call each other donkeys just as we do. I know that.——When I am a millionaire I'll erect a monument to God.——Imagine the future as a milkshake with sugar and cinnamon. One fellow upsets it and howls, another stirs it all together and sweats. Why not skim off the cream?——Or don't you believe that one can learn how?

ERNEST.

Let us skim!

HANS.

What remains the hens will eat.——I have pulled my head out of so many traps already——

ERNEST.

Let us skim, Hans!——Why do you laugh?

HANS.

Are you beginning again already?

ERNEST.

But one of us must begin.

HANS.

Thirty years from now, on some evening like to-day, if we recall this one, perhaps it will seem too beautiful for expression.

ERNEST.

And how everything springs from self!

HANS.

Why not?

ERNEST.

If by chance one were alone——one might like to weep!

HANS.

Don't let us be sad! (*He kisses him on the mouth.*)

ERNEST.

(*Returning the kiss.*)
I left the house with the idea of just speaking to you and turning back again.

HANS.

I waited for you.——Virtue is not a bad garment, but it requires an imposing figure.

ERNEST.

It fits us loosely as yet.——I should not have been content if I had not met you.——I love you, Hans, as I have never loved a soul——

HANS.

Let us not be sad.——If we recall this in thirty years, perhaps we shall make fun of it.——And yet everything is so beautiful. The mountains glow; the grapes hang before our mouths and the evening breeze caresses the rocks like a playful flatterer.——

SCENE SEVENTH.

A clear November night. The dry foliage of the bushes and trees rustles. Torn clouds chase each other beneath the moon——Melchior clambers over the churchyard wall.

MELCHIOR.

(*Springing down inside.*)
The pack won't follow me here.——While they are searching the brothels I can get my breath and discover how much I have accomplished.
Coat in tatters, pockets empty——I'm not safe from the most harmless.—
—I must try to get deeper into the wood to-morrow.

I have trampled down a cross——Even to-day the flowers are frozen!——
The earth is cold all around——

In the domain of the dead!——

To climb out of the hole in the roof was not as hard as this road!——It was
only there that I kept my presence of mind——

I hung over the abyss——everything was lost in it, vanished——Oh, if I
could have stayed there.

Why she, on my account!——Why not the guilty!——Inscrutable providence!—
—I would have broken stones and gone hungry!——What is to keep me
straight now?——Offense follows offense. I am swallowed up in the
morass. I haven't strength left to get out of it——

I was not bad!——I was not bad!——I was not bad!——No mortal ever
wandered so dejectedly over graves before.——Pah!——I won't lose
courage! Oh, if I should go crazy——during this very night!

I must seek there among the latest ones!——The wind pipes on every
stone in a different key——an anguishing symphony!——The decayed
wreaths rip apart and swing with their long threads in bits about the marble crosses——A wood of scarecrows!——Scarecrows on every grave,
each more gruesome than the other——as high as houses, from which
the devil runs away.——The golden letters sparkle so coldly——The
weeping willows groan and move their giant fingers over the inscriptions—
—

A praying angel——a tablet.

The clouds throw their shadows over it.——How the wind hurries and
howls!——Like the march of an army it drives in from the east.——Not
a star in the heavens——

Evergreen in the garden plot?——Evergreen?——A maiden——

HERE RESTS IN GOD

Wendla Bergmann, born May 5, 1878,

died from Cholorosis,

October 27, 1892.

Blessed are the Pure of Heart

And I am her murderer. I am her murderer!——Despair is left me——I
dare not weep here. Away from here!——Away——

MORITZ STIEFEL.

(*With his head under his arm, comes stamping over the graves.*)
A moment, Melchior! The opportunity will not occur so readily again. You
   can't guess what depends upon the place and the time——

MELCHIOR.

Where do you come from?

MORITZ.

From over there——over by the wall. You knocked down my cross. I lie by
   the wall.——Give me your hand, Melchior.——

MELCHIOR.

You are not Moritz Stiefel!

MORITZ.

Give me your hand. I am convinced you will thank me. It won't be so
   easy again! This is an unusually fortunate encounter.——I came out
   especially——

MELCHIOR.

Don't you sleep?

MORITZ.

Not what you call sleep.——We sit on the church-tower, on the high gables
   of the roof——wherever we please.——

MELCHIOR.

Restless?

MORITZ.

Half happy.——We wander among the Mayflowers, among the lonely paths
   in the woods. We hover over gatherings of people, over the scene of
   accidents, gardens, festivals.——We cower in the chimneys of dwelling-
   places and behind the bed curtains.——Give me your hand.——We
   don't associate with each other, but we see and hear everything that is
   going on in the world. We know that everything is stupidity, everything
   that men do and contend for, and we laugh at it.

MELCHIOR.

What good does that do?

MORITZ.

What good does it have to do?——We are fit for nothing more, neither good nor evil. We stand high, high above earthly beings—each for himself alone. We do not associate with each other, because it would bore us. Not one of us cares for anything which he might lose. We are indifferent both to sorrow and to joy. We are satisfied with ourselves and that is all. We despise the living so heartily that we can hardly pity them. They amuse us with their doings, because, being alive, they are not worthy of compassion. We laugh at their tragedies—each by himself——and make reflections upon them.——Give me your hand! If you give me your hand, you will fall down with laughter over the sensation which made you give me your hand.

MELCHIOR.

Doesn't that disgust you?

MORITZ.

We are too high for that. We smile!——At my burial I was among the mourners. I had a right good time. That is sublimity, Melchior! I howled louder than any and slunk over to the wall to hold my belly from shaking with laughter. Our unapproachable sublimity is the only viewpoint which the trash understands——They would have laughed at me also before I swung myself off.

MELCHIOR.

I have no desire to laugh at myself.

MORITZ.

The living, as such, are not really worth compassion!——I admit I should not have thought so either. And now it is incomprehensible to me how one can be so naïve. I see through the fraud so clearly that not a cloud remains.——Why do you want to loiter now, Melchior! Give me your hand! In the turn of a head you will stand heaven high above yourself.——Your life is a sin of omission——

MELCHIOR.

Can you forget?

MORITZ.

We can do everything. Give me your hand! We can pity the young, who take their timidity for idealism, and the old, who break their hearts from stoical deliberation. We see the Kaiser tremble at a scurrilous ballad and the lazzaroni before the youngest policeman. We ignore the masks of comedians and see the poet in the shadow of the mask. We see happiness in beggars' rags and the capitalist in misery and toil. We observe lovers and see them blush before each other, foreseeing that they are deceived deceivers. We see parents bringing children into the world that they may be able to say to them: "How happy you are to have such parents!"——and see the children go and do likewise. We can observe the innocent girl in the qualms of her first love, and the five-groschen harlot reading Schiller.——We see God and the devil blaming each other, and cherish the unspeakable belief that both of them are drunk——Peace and joy, Melchior! You only need to reach me your little finger. You may become snow-white before you have such a favorable opportunity again!

MELCHIOR.

If I gave you my hand, Moritz, it would be from self-contempt.——I see myself outlawed. What lent me courage lies in the grave. I can no longer consider noble emotions as worthy.——And see nothing, nothing, that can save me now from my degradation.——To myself I am the most contemptible creature in the universe.

MORITZ.

What delays you?——
(*A masked man appears.*)

THE MASKED MAN.

(*To Melchior.*)
You are trembling from hunger. You are not fit to judge. (*To Moritz.*) You go!

MELCHIOR.

Who are you?

THE MASKED MAN.

I refuse to tell. (*To Moritz.*) Vanish!——What business have you here!——
Why haven't you on your head?

MORITZ.

I shot myself.

THE MASKED MAN.

Then stay where you belong. You are done with! Don't annoy us here with
your stink of the grave. It's inconceivable!——Look at your fingers! Pfu,
the devil! They will crumble soon.

MORITZ.

Please don't send me away——

MELCHIOR.

Who are you, sir??

MORITZ.

Please don't send me away. Please don't. Let me stay here a bit with you; I
won't disturb you in anything——It is so dreadful down there.

THE MASKED MAN.

Why do you gabble about sublimity, then?——You know that that is
humbug——sour grapes! Why do you lie so diligently, you chimera? If
you consider it so great a favor, you may stay, as far as I am concerned.
But take yourself to leeward, my dear friend——and please keep your
dead man's hand out of the game!

MELCHIOR.

Will you tell me once for all who you are, or not?

THE MASKED MAN.

No——I propose to you that you shall confide yourself to me. I will take care of your future success.

MELCHIOR.

You are——my father?

THE MASKED MAN.

Wouldn't you know your father by his voice?

MELCHIOR.

No.

THE MASKED MAN.

Your father seeks consolation at this moment in the sturdy arms of your mother.——I will open the world to you. Your momentary lack of resolution springs from your miserable condition. With a warm supper inside of you, you will make fun of it.

MELCHIOR.

(*To himself.*)
It can only be the devil! (*Aloud.*) After that of which I have been guilty, a warm supper cannot give me back my peace!

THE MASKED MAN.

That will follow the supper!——I can tell you this much, the girl had better have given birth. She was built properly. Unfortunately, she was killed by the abortives given by Mother Schmidt.——I will take you out among men. I will give you the opportunity to enlarge your horizon fabulously. I will make you thoroughly acquainted with everything interesting that the world has to offer.

MELCHIOR.

Who are you? Who are you?——I can't trust a man that I don't know.

THE MASKED MAN.

You can't learn to know me unless you trust me.

MELCHIOR.

Do you think so?

THE MASKED MAN.

Of course!——Besides, you have no choice.

MELCHIOR.

I can reach my hand to my friend here at any moment.

THE MASKED MAN.

Your friend is a charlatan. Nobody laughs who has a pfennig left in cash. The sublime humorist is the most miserable, most pitiable creature in creation.

MELCHIOR.

Let the humorist be what he may; you tell me who you are, or I'll reach the humorist my hand.

THE MASKED MAN.

What then?

MORITZ.

He is right, Melchior. I have boasted. Take his advice and profit by it. No matter how masked he is——he is, at least.

MELCHIOR.

Do you believe in God?

THE MASKED MAN.

Yes, conditionally.

MELCHIOR.

Will you tell me who discovered gunpowder?

THE MASKED MAN.

Berthold Schwarz——alias Konstantin Anklitzen.——A Franciscan monk at Freiburg in Breisgau, in 1330.

MORITZ.

What wouldn't I give if he had let it alone!

THE MASKED MAN.

You would only have hanged yourself then.

MELCHIOR.

What do you think about morals?

THE MASKED MAN.

You rascal, am I your schoolboy?

MELCHIOR.

Do I know what you are?

MORITZ.

Don't quarrel!——Please don't quarrel. What good does that do?——Why should we sit, two living men and a corpse, together in a churchyard at two o'clock in the morning if we want to quarrel like topers! It will be a pleasure to me to arbitrate between you. If you want to quarrel, I'll take my head under my arm and go!

MELCHIOR.

You are the same old 'fraid cat as ever.

THE MASKED MAN.

The phantom is not wrong. One shouldn't forget one's dignity.——By morals I understand the real product of two imaginary quantities. The imaginary quantities are "shall" and "will." The product is called morals and leaves no doubt of its reality.

MORITZ.

If you had only told me that earlier! My morals hounded me to death. For the sake of my dear parents I killed myself. "Honor thy father and mother that thy days may be long in the land." The text made a phenomenal fool of me.

THE MASKED MAN.

Give yourself up to no more illusions, dear friend. Your dear parents would have died as little from it as you did. Judged righteously, they would only have raged and stormed from the healthiest necessity.

MELCHIOR.

That may be right as far as it goes.——I can assure you, however, sir, that if I reach Moritz my hand, sooner or later my morals alone will have to bear the blame.

THE MASKED MAN.

That is just the reason you are not Moritz!

MORITZ.

But I don't believe the difference is so material, so compulsive at least, esteemed unknown, but what by chance the same thing might have happened to you as happened to me that time when I trotted through the alder grove with a pistol in my pocket.

THE MASKED MAN.

Don't you remember me? You have been standing for the moment actually between life and death.——Moreover, in my opinion, this is not exactly the place in which to continue such a profound debate.

MORITZ.

Certainly, it's growing cold, gentlemen! They dressed me in my Sunday suit, but I wear neither undershirt nor drawers.

MELCHIOR.

Farewell, dear Moritz. I don't know where the man is taking me. But he is a man——

MORITZ.

Don't blame me for seeking to kill you, Melchior. It was old attachment. All my life I shall only be able to complain and lament that I cannot accompany you once more.

THE MASKED MAN.

At the end everyone has his part——You the consoling consciousness of having nothing——you an enervating doubt of everything.—Farewell.

MELCHIOR.

Farewell, Moritz. Take my heartfelt thanks for appearing before me again. How many former bright days have we lived together during the fourteen years! I promise you, Moritz, come what may, whether during the coming years I become ten times another, whether I prosper or fail, I shall never forget you——

MORITZ.

Thanks, thanks, dear friend.

MELCHIOR.

——and when at last I am an old man with gray hair, then, perhaps, you will again stand closer to me than all those living about me.

MORITZ.

I thank you. Good luck to your journey, gentlemen. Do not delay any longer.

THE MASKED MAN.

Come, child! (*He lays his arm upon that of Melchior and disappears with him over the graves.*)

MORITZ.

(*Alone.*)

Now I sit here with my head under my arm.——The moon covers her face, unveils herself again and seems not a hair the cleverer.——I will go back to my place, right my cross, which that madcap trampled down so inconsiderately, and when everything is in order I will lie down on my back again, warm myself in the corruption and smile.

Printed in Great Britain
by Amazon

38352718R00067